Henry Howe

Odds and Ends

Containing queer happenings to men and things of our time, after Noah came out

of the ark

Henry Howe

Odds and Ends
Containing queer happenings to men and things of our time, after Noah came out of the ark

ISBN/EAN: 9783337325589

Printed in Europe, USA, Canada, Australia, Japan

Cover: Foto ©Lupo / pixelio.de

More available books at **www.hansebooks.com**

ODDS AND ENDS,

CONTAINING

Queer Happenings to Men and Things of our Time, after Noah came out of the Ark.

" A little NONSENSE now and then,
Is relished by the WISEST men ;"
While FOOLS, with yawning maws for more,
Can cram from our abundant store.

Illustrated by sixty imaginary pictures, with FRAMES ready furnished.

DEDICATED, by Special Permission, TO FOOLS, and designed for issue on ALL FOOLS' DAY, but it "Hung Fire."

A Medley of Caricatures,

Seen in a Vision.

BY DR. ALATE WIDEAWAKE,

Amateur Dreamer, Honorary Member of the Society for the Infusion of Useful Knowledge on the Cachinnatory System.

CINCINNATI:
PUBLISHED BY R. W. CARROLL & CO.
1868.

TO

Odds and Ends,

CONTAINING

Queer Happenings.

"I DO N'T UNDERSTAND this book," the reader, on his first opening, will exclaim.

Of course he do n't!

It is more than could be expected!

To be honest, the author has serious doubts if he does *himself!*

Many a child is a surprise to its father, an astonishment to its mother, and an enigma to every body. But, nevertheless, being a child, it requires to be fathered and mothered, and then in due time swung off, thenceforth to oscillate for itself.

The theory is a dream, in which the past and the present are thrown together, and real characters and mythological characters introduced, and meet Noah and his family as they come out of the Ark. The latter are not the personages of the genuine history, but such as were seen in the vision. Why the dream should have as a basis the advent of Noah from the Ark, is explained in the first two introductory pages; and the originating incident is true. The general alluded to was the noble-hearted Burnside.

We imagine the good parson, as "the MUG" of his old parishioner was thus unexpectedly sent to him, indulged in "a SMILE." As he was not a resident of *Maine*, he was not de*bar*red from it.

Just before the vision, the dreamer heard the music of Carl Rosa and Madame Parepa. What more natural than that their sweet notes should run through his dream, and that, too, generally in the form of apt poetical quotations?

The *imaginary pictures*, at first view, will puzzle all. What are shown are frames or borders for scenes which the reader may imagine. Few will have the artistic talent for it, and none are expected to do so. Introduced as a novelty, they serve, with the annexed descriptions, to give an idea of the contents of the work.

"What an incongruous mixture!" some will say. "True," we reply. Dreams are always incongruous. Beside, our aim is humor. Humor is said never to exist without incongruity. It arises from placing things and ideas in false relations. It can't be defined. We thus illustrate it:

Nearly forty years since, the venerable President Day, of Yale, and a young student were alone together in a stage-coach, passing from New Haven to Hartford. A sudden smile flitting across the face of the grave teacher, aroused the curiosity of the young man, and, on looking out of the window, he in turn smiled, for he saw the cause. In the center of a corn-field was the effigy of a man on a pole as a scarecrow, on top of which was calmly perching, in unconscious innocence of the incongruity of his resting-place, one of the blackest of crows!

THE KEY TO ODDS AND ENDS. C

Humor is permitted in a sin-abounding world, and doubtless for wise purposes. Six days in a week, even a Christian can laugh!
But humor can have no place above, for

"Order is Heaven's first law."

Where order reigns supreme, incongruity can not exist. Yet so keen is the sense of order in some pharisaical individuals, so anxious are they even here to anticipate, that they ever walk our streets with solemn visages, and gauge personal piety by the length of the countenance—not by that spirit of universal love which wells up warm from the heart, and smiles in joy at the happiness of the most insignificant created thing.

Humor being allowed with us below, we have endeavored to press it into good service.

The book is in opposition to what is termed in irony the Democratic party. No one outside of a lunatic asylum can believe that name is claimed in any other sense by an organization that has marked its track in blood, and seeks its elevation by crushing the weak, the lowly, and the ignorant. Our moral is that we must protect the poor and the humble of this earth, and that only by so doing can we be truly happy. This moral is shadowed forth in chapters H and I, and developed in the last.

Many things are caricatured; much by-play indulged in. If the reader, in certain places, sees no hits, he must conclude none are there intended. Some public personages for whom we have a heart-felt regard are thrown into amusing relations; but not as strongly as others, especially that unwholesome individual at the head of our Government, who, for three years past, has disturbed the peace of our country and thwarted the will of this great people.

Some minds will enjoy this book; perhaps a majority may turn from it with repulsion. That is no reason why it should not be published.

D THE KEY TO ODDS AND ENDS.

"Find out," said an old man, once on a time, "what is public opinion; then act squarely against it, and, in nine cases out of ten, you will act right!"

The taste of that select few should be gratified, who can

READ with believing hearts the Travels of Baron Munchausen!

REGARD with chivalrous emotions the wondrous exploits of Don Quixote!

REVEL in the picturesque scenes experienced by the renowned Doctor Syntax!

DELIGHT in the Adventures of Lemuel Gulliver!

ESTEEM Parson Weems as the Prince of Biographers!

LISTEN with rapture to the narrative of Sinbad the Sailor!

ENTERTAIN a profound respect for the venerable character of our oldest inhabitant, the Wandering Jew!

APPRECIATE the lucubrations of the author of the Devil on Two Sticks!

BASK in the effulgence of Petroleum Nasby!

CACHINATE under the scintillations of Artemus!

ADMIRE love sonnets to the mermaid of Barnum!

SYMPATHIZE with Japheth in Search of his Father!

DRINK in with tittilating nerves the entrancing Melodies of Mother Goose!

LEAN forward with keen appetite to the juicy carvings of the Fat Contributor. And then

PANT for a hot stew from the bivalve establishment kept by Holmes' tall young oysterman, "down below!"

H. H.

CINCINNATI, O., 1868.

CONTENTS.

	PAGE.
The Author's Curve of Courtesy and Acquaintance..................	7
The Publisher's Curve of Courtesy and Apology.....................	27

CHAPTER A.
Introduces the United States Moses, All Gammon, Lemuel Gulliver, Sinbad the Sailor, Baron Munchhausen, the Wandering Jew, with original anecdotes of the same............................... 39

CHAPTER B.
Describes how Mr. Noah was extricated from an unpleasant little happening by Andy, Secretaries Sewap and McKashlock, General Grent, Ben Botlaw, and others; the discovery of Chicago; auction of George Francis Fastline................... 47

CHAPTER C.
Describes the Pendletum Currency, and what befell those who went up in their financial balloon............................... 57

CHAPTER D.
Discovery of Mr. Noah's boots on the Pacific Railroad in the Rocky Mountains, with anecdotes of the Noahs........................ 67

CHAPTER E.
Mrs. Noah receives an invitation to go through Mr. Stewat's dry goods establishment by railroad; Harry Wood Beachem, a young journeyman preacher, and author of blue-covered literature, appears.. 83

CONTENTS.

CHAPTER F.
Describes the multitude who met the Noahs as they came out of the Ark—as Wendell Feelups, Agagassy, Mr. Van Winkle, Max Marattlezak, the companies of "Mutual Friends," "Odd Friends," "Ye Gods and Little Fishes," "Uncle Sam's Men," "Ye Dickens Squad," and the Mewonica.................... 91

CHAPTER G.
The Grand Gala, where various catastrophies happen to Andy, and he finally is killed, and then restored to life by the Awful Unknown with his serpent wand.................................... 115

CHAPTER H.
Mr. Dickens has a good time under a big sugar-maple, sings a song, and is finally captured by Mrs. Grundy, and talks with her... 137

CHAPTER I.
Mr. Dickens continues his benevolent talk with Mrs. Grundy, and it is shown fools can yet say, "We live!"........................ 151

CHAPTER J.
Mr. Dickens prepares to give a reading.............................. 163

CHAPTER K.
The Awful Unknown sets loose the animals of the Ark, when they charge upon the crowd, who run in terror, and many strange things happen... 173

CHAPTER L.
Andy departs for Tennessee, escorted by the corps of Odd Friends and an apparition in the sky; the author awakes............... 187

CHAPTER M.
Burlesque and satire dropped, and the reader led to pause and reflect, "What are we?" "Where do we stand?" "Whither are we tending?"... 207

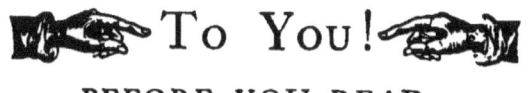

To You!

BEFORE YOU READ.

DR. ALATE WIDEAWAKE

HIS CURVE OF COURTESY AND ACQUAINTANCE

AND

"How do You do?"

"A DREAM, but not all a DREAM," and this the way of it. On a day we opened a drawer for paper on which to write a letter to a friend, when we exhumed some sheets buried since our Sunny brethren failed in their attempt to tear away from the embraces of their kind uncle. Those sheets were adorned with the patriotic pictures in brilliant illuminations, peculiar to that period. As we glanced over the devices we smiled. It seemed centuries since we had used such, and our life now so different, our daily sensations so different, that we felt queer. It was like a glimpse of a forgotten existence in another world in which we once lived.

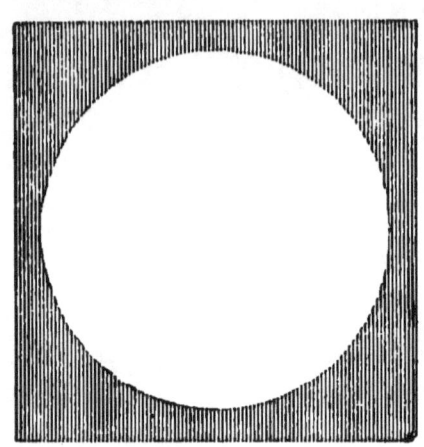

IMAGINARY PICTURE.

Dr. Wideawake rummaging that drawer.

We selected a sheet luminous with the fierce-whiskered portrait of a general, once a parishioner of our friend; the latter, as you thus perceive, of that estimable class of citizens who, arrayed in white gowns one day in seven, perch behind little boxes and talk to people to make them good and happy. We placed at the end this sentence, for we felt it:

"*P. S. Above is the portrait of a man who met Noah when he came out of the ark.*"

On an evening we attended a concert of

those charming artistes, Carl Rosa and Madame Parepa, and, at its close, went to a social of a good deacon's, who always gives a generous "spread." We are not so abusive to hospitality as to neglect creature comforts when painstakingly prepared for us, nor so unamiable to our own appetites as to turn the cold shoulder to their moderate requests. So we did our duty as was becoming one who felt he had a part to perform in life, and before the wee small hours arrived, were in our proper place in horizontal position, our external senses deprived of their whereabouts.

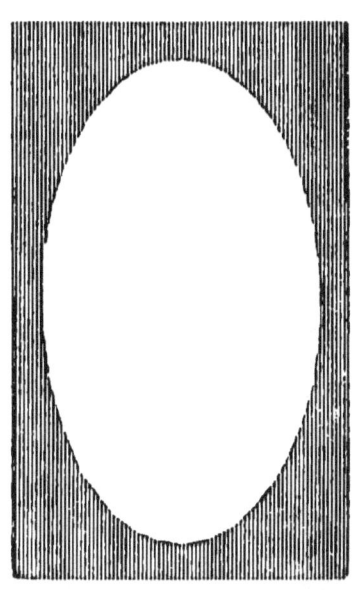

IMAGINARY PICTURE.

Carl Rosa as he plays upon the violin, and Madame Parepa while she sings.

We dreamed, and the result is these revelations, just as All Gammon breathed them into our ears. Carl Rosa and Madame Parepa were also present, and we had their music interspersed through the narrative, and without expense. Should they, consequently, make any drafts upon us, we will try and honor the same.

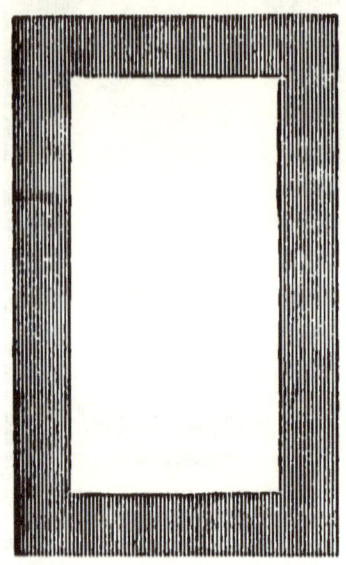

IMAGINARY PICTURE.
The good Deacon's "Spread."

The immediate cause of our visions was evidently in the good Deacon's fried oysters. We had often heard of oysters being *coppery*, but this was our first experience. We must have swallowed some *copperheads!* We know it, for we saw snakes! and in it, too, the biggest copperhead of all; that awful one who, from an early day, has walked the earth,

> " To see how his stock goes on,
> And switched his long tail,
> As a gentleman switches his cane."

You will perceive that most of the personages we saw in our vision are mere myths. General Grent is a myth! Secretary Sewap is a myth! Secretary Stunem is a myth! So is Grandmamma Wulles, Jefferson Devis, Baron Munchausen, and the Wandering Jew! Nobody ever heard of them before! All Gammon is not a myth! Every body, even the children in the streets, know him.

Sinbad the Sailor can't be a myth, for in our boy days we saw a sloop in New Haven harbor which had the words "The Dragon" on its stern, which a sailor aboard told us Sinbad once commanded; also a snuff-box, in the hands of an old sea pensioner, at Sailor's Snug Harbor, on Staten Island, who said it originally belonged to Sinbad. It was doubtless the one thus herein poetically described:

"His Love a *pewter* snuff-box had,
And left him when she died."

The snuff-box this old sea-dog had was *pewter!* He had years before given up his water life, and there was no chip big enough to tempt him to it again.

"Old ships, in time,
Must be out of commission,
Nor again weigh anchor,
Yo! heave, O!"

Lemuel Gulliver is not a myth, for we were once in a fishing-smack off Gull Island, in Long Island Sound, and aboard was a venerable sea-faring man, known as "Old Sou'-

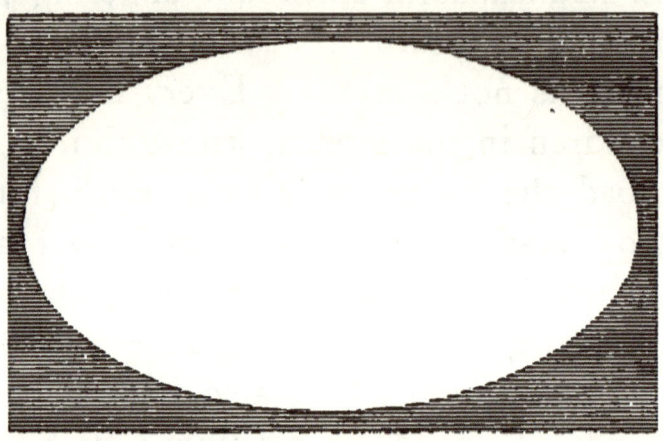

IMAGINARY PICTURE.

Mr. Sou'-wester making that vegetable deposit upon the nose of sleeping innocence.

wester," who had the rheumatism badly, and was universally respected. He was born on the ocean, cradled on its waves, and fed on hard-tack from the gum stage up. He made an appetizing chowder, the memory of which is a delicious thing which we shall not sell for any of your *Pendletum* currency. He told us Lemuel taught him the art; so we know Lemuel is not a myth.

When Sou'-wester thus informed us, he cocked up his eyes, opened his mouth, and presenting his check to that depository, drew therefrom a moist vegetable deposit; then giving the waistband of his under-rigging a hitch, he balanced himself on his left leg, and, with surprising accuracy and force, threw it at a feminine beauty that lay in sleeping innocence on the deck. It struck square on the point of her smelling arrangement, when she sprang as if shot, curled her tail under her, yelped " Ki yi, ki yi," darted off, and, in a twinkling, had disappeared down the hatchway.

Seven gentlemen, amateur fishermen, from New Haven, had just seated themselves around a table in the cabin for dinner. They were ravenous, for they had been off in the yawl fishing since sunrise, without any thing to eat, and it was then four o'clock in the afternoon. Their table was bountifully spread with good things; plenty of liquors, and, in the center, an immense dish of one of Sou'-wester's famous chowders. The terror-stricken female, on arriving at the head of the hatchway, appears to have forgotten (indeed, if she ever knew) the prudent maxim, "Look before you leap." She gave a terrific spring, and, for a moment, was in no particular place, but was going to one quick. She appears to have

IMAGINARY PICTURE.

Consternation of the amateurs on the advent of the In-got, and the anguish of the In-got.

been billed for the chowder dish, for she landed plump in it just at the identical moment that one of the amateurs had removed the cover to help around, and they were all looking on in eager anticipation. The chowder dish, the chowder itself, the liquors, glasses, and every thing else on that table, were thereby broken, and mixed, and scattered in one confused mass. Oh! it was a grievous matter for the amateurs, so totally were they unprepared for such an oc-*cur*-rence! It was a hard fact in life that had struck them in a tender spot. It was none of your light, flimsy, PENDLETUM CUR-RENCY, but a solid INGOT!

On recovering from their consternation, one of the anguished, *kindly*, *very kindly*, took that female by the handle, and *slowly*, *very slowly*, walked up the hatchway to the lee side of the vessel, and bending over *gently*, *very gently*, for he was a humane amateur, deposited her in a *wet, very wet*,

IMAGINARY PICTURE.
The deposit of the In-got in a wet, very wet place.

place, and she has not *written* to her friends since!

We should not speak of such a painful matter for fear of unnecessarily harrowing your feelings, but our veracity might be questioned by some unamiable persons, of which this world, alas! is too full, as regards this man Sou'wester, and the relation of this incident might possibly recall him to the recollection of those knowing these circumstances, or of somebody that did know of such as could tell them of some folks that might have done so, if they wanted to.

It so happens that six of the seven gentlemen present were over forty years since gathered to their mothers.* We are not expected to call upon them! The name of the seventh we don't recollect. We only know he was in the Educatory Corps of Yale. Some colleges do have Educatory Corps. He was in the

---

* What Dr. Wideawake means by the expression "gathered to their mothers," is not clear. Perhaps they had someway got into trouble, and, sorrowing, gone and hid their heads in their mamma's aprons.—*The Publisher*.

Botany part—was a Professor, and attended to a Herbarium of Greek Roots.

Fortunately, though, two gentlemen were on deck and saw Mr. Sou'wester make that vegetable deposit, and, if living, we might call upon them as vouchers, for we take a just pride in mentioning their names as among acquaintances of those who might know us by hearsay, if they should try and find out somebody that thought they could learn of any people that ever did. We say we take a just pride in mentioning their names, viz.: Rock Hotchkiss, Esq., and Mr. Fry. The latter had a rural residence under the brow of Pine Rock, later got a situation in the Eleemosynary Institution of the town, where, we believe, he did all that could have been expected of him, giving general satisfaction, for he was a good boarder, and always walked every plank he trod upon in a commendatory manner.

Mr. Fry's rural residence was once a great resort of citizens and strangers, to view its architectural proportions, and enjoy the charms of his conversation. His place went by the name of *Fry's Cave;* why, though, we never could see. It wa'n't much of a hole. It was quarried off, and used in the building of the Long Wharf in New Haven.

IMAGINARY PICTURE.

Mr. Fry's Rural Residence.

Jedediah Morse, in his geography, the first edition of which was published in 1784, says: "This is the longest wharf in the United States." It is rendered necessary "because the harbor is gradually filling up with mud." We are happy to say that harbor, to this day, continues in the line of duty—"is gradually filling up with mud." It is soothing to see how quiet, regular, every thing goes on in "the *land* of steady habits"—even *off* shore. The contemplation somehow reconciles one to the hard facts in life—while the soft facts seem more pleasing than ever.

Rock Hotchkiss, Esq., lived in Hotchkisstown, under West Rock. He was a remarkable individual. What his Christian name was we never knew—we do n't think anybody ever did, unless it was his grandmother. He *went*, and perhaps may have also *returned*, by his mineralogical name. It was Rock. Early in life he tumbled off West Rock, which has a perpendicular of trap of nearly one hundred feet. Ever after his name was thus mineralogical, and because he gave such an interesting history of his sensations while falling. He stated soon as he found he was on the way, he was in *perfect* agony to get there—it seemed to him as though he never should reach bottom.

When he was in the air, going! going! going! Mr. Hotchkiss's sufferings could not be called the agony of *suspense*, but what might be termed the *dropping* agony; and when he arrived, he had the worst agony of all—the *stopping* agony. Oh! it was dreadful! Had he been a bird, he would have been spared suffering. Nobody ever blamed him because he was not a bird. He got thereby what we all desire in life—a solid name among his neighbors. We don't believe he ever wrote folly to relieve the sad hours of any body. He wouldn't see the wisdom of it. If ever he did write, it was about something substantial as the everlasting hills.

IMAGINARY PICTURE.

Rock Hotchkiss, Esq.

Rock Hotchkiss had an incident with a rabbit. One day he was in the woods setting his traps, when he espied an immense snow-white rabbit wedged between two branches. He caught the animal, and at once started for his home with it under his arms.

In the joy of his heart, he talked to it in a loving manner as he walked, just as though it understood him. Stroking the rabbit, he said:

"Poor pussy! what a beautiful, plump little fellow you are!

"You are the finest rabbit I ever saw!

"I always was fond of rabbits!

"They are the best eating in the world!

"I'll dress you, and get Mrs. Hotchkiss to stew you!

"No, I won't; I'll be hanged if I do! you'll be better broiled!

"I'll have a hot fire, have you split open, put on a gridiron, and thoroughly cooked brown and nice!

"And then you shall be brought on to the table, well peppered and salted, and buttered with the best of butter.

"And then Mrs. Hotchkiss and I will draw up our chairs and ——"

Just as he got to this point, his face, all aglow with the ecstasy of anticipation, smacking his lips, and his inner man sympathizing with this outer expression, he inadvertently lifted up his arm, when that rabbit took a *mean advantage*—sprang away from him—darted off!

For the moment, Rock Hotchkiss, Esq.,

stood like a man who had just got an idea. He threw his head back, and raised up his hands. But it was for a moment, for Rock was a philosopher. He seized the hard facts of life on their smooth sides.

IMAGINARY PICTURE.

Rock Hotchkiss, Esq., as he looked when he sent that message after the rabbit.

He changed his position, leaned his head and body forward, and bringing the palms of his hands on his knees, looked steadily at the fast vanishing form of his lost one, with an expression as if of annihilation; and, as he looked, he fiercely grated out between his teeth this message, and sent it over the line after him:

"Go! ye little, miserable, wooly-tailed cus! Go! *ye aint wuth the butter 't would take to cook ye!*"

The Noahs are not myths. The good book tells us about them, but don't tell us they had girls. They didn't have any. It was a great mistake in the family arrangements. Girls are useful! Useful to dust the parlor, read novels, thump the piano, walk the streets, and to call upon the paternal parent for funds to pay for tickets to the rink. We shall always speak well of the girls. Our mother was once one of 'em; but that was a long time ago, and she couldn't help herself; it was before she saw the ancient gentleman, and we, therefore, don't lay it up seriously against her.

Andy Jinsin is not a myth, but an actual reality. We know it, for we voted for him, and been happy ever since at the thought we did it.

His Satanic Majesty is not a myth. Jawge H. Pendletum is not a myth—can't be a myth —mustn't be a myth; there is a *dreadful necessity for his existence!*

From the strange, crooked goings on in this country the last two years,

> Don't every body say,
> "The d——l's to pay!"

We are in favor of paying our honest debts; and as, by common consent, this wicked wretch is our great creditor, we must give him his due. But as he will make bad use of the money, we throw up our hats for paying him in the most spavined currency that can be raised. Pendletum is the man to raise it for us—the only man. Trot him out! Three cheers and a tiger for Pendletum!

Dreams have been published before. Don't "the Book of books" contain visions and dreams? Why, it all ends in a dream! But we have an advantage: our dream can be mostly interpreted, for it reflects

> "The living manners as they rise."

We said "we dreamed a dream, but it was not all a dream." We did; but all the dream we have not told. We dreamed some things so wonderful that we should tremble to relate them, for fear that none would believe that we dreamed them. It would be unwise to do so; would so hurt us on a point where we feel peculiarly tender—tarnish our reputation for *veracity!*

* * * * * * * * * * * * * *

The Publisher's Curve of Courtesy and Apology to You.

A PAINFUL INCIDENT occurred when Dr. Alate Wideawake was last in our office, which prevented him from explaining some apparent incongruities in his vision, and also from making his intended curve of courtesy and farewell. We have not seen nor heard of him since, and fear some accident may have befallen him.

There was a rumor, though we can trace it to no reliable source, that he had gone "abroad"—went on a mission—appointed "Charge de

Affairs" among the Hottentots. Perhaps Andy may have appointed him. He did much for the "elevation" of Andy: held *the bottle* the day he was inaugurated. It was necessary that Andy should sign a document, and Alate held the *ink* bottle. Andy signed his name, and put a circle around it, to indicate that he was going to be a circumference, which he has been: and felt as though he was in the straightest of all lines in being a circumference.

We do think Andy has sent him to the Hottentots. What makes us think it true is that the Sandy Hook Pilots just in, bring word they met one hundred miles and two rods out at sea a scow filled with passengers bound for the "other side." Dr. Alate Wideawake may have been one of those passengers. We think he was—indeed are certain he was. Where else can he be?

As Doctor Wideawake is thus absent, and we know, absolutely know, gone on a mission —for have we not proved it?—it becomes us to explain some apparent incongruities in his book.

Now first he speaks of that picture as making him feel as though it was the portrait of a man who *met* Noah when he came out of the Ark. We all of us say when we see any thing much antiquated, "it looks as though it came *out* of the Ark." We feel this, and so say it. But Doctor Wideawake has a logical mind. He knew there were no generals in the Ark, at any rate not any of our Uncle Samuel's generals; at the same time he felt as though this general lived as far back as that time, and so wrote to his clerical friend.

The entire dream is full of incongruities; but only think, though, what poor Wideawake had swallowed!—and how he must have suffered! It was enough to make any body have incongruous dreams. Now it is all out of him, we hope he will keep at more sober business.

The Noah family, as dreamed about by him, are much like the old-fashioned New England Yankees, as they were when he was a boy, and dovetailed and mixed into matters and things, and human beings considerably every-where on Uncle Sam's farm at the present time.

We think, if Doctor Wideawake had remained in his native Connecticut, his dreams would have been regular and methodical, as dreams usually are. Our apology is that he has lived more than twenty years in the West, among that barbarous, rude people, and so has become woefully degenerated.

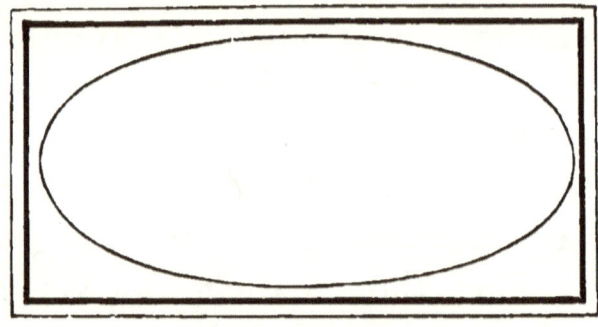

IMAGINARY PICTURE.

Doctor Wideawake seen taking Ben Would's paper instrumentally.

Were it not for the Atlantic Monthly, the Tribune, and the Independent, which he has always taken regularly, together with piscatorial consignments from Cape Cod, for family use, we believe nothing could have saved him from utter wreck. He did once take Ben Would's paper, not regularly, but instrumentally. It was only once: and the instrument, a *pair of tongs!*

The Doctor told us that although he has written these revelations as being whispered in his ears by All Gammon, this explanation must not be taken literally. He was, in fact, spiritually possessed by him, and saw as with All Gammon's own eyes, and heard as with All Gammon's own ears, and smelt as with All Gammon's own nose, every thing that transpired, hence he is enabled to give such vivid descriptions. How such a thing could happen is mysterious. Later in the age of the world it is to be hoped the chemistry of spiritual infusion and transmutation will be better understood. For the present, we must, in these matters, pull in our oars, and let the water drip from their ends until we obtain new revelations. In the meanwhile, as we rest, we will just ask the steersman to hand over for our thirsty throats such spiritual refreshment as he has already stowed away, tightly corked, in the little box under his seat.

When the Doctor had his composition ready for the press, he felt keenly the necessity of having it all just right. He would not lightly present to the public a work of such a weighty

IMAGINARY PICTURE.

Dr. Wideawake is seen submitting the manuscript of this work to a town meeting of citizens for their approval.

import. He sent the town crier through the streets, with a bell, and at the corners with a loud "Oh, yes! Oh, yes!" the citizens were summoned at a public meeting to hear it read paragraph by paragraph, and to vote upon each separately. In most cases they voted an unanimous approval. In others much dissent ensued, and angry and vociferous discussion, ending with several unhappy knockdowns, which grieved the good Doctor, who is tender-hearted to a fault, most sorely. These disturbing points were finally settled by a division of the house, and a counting of hands.

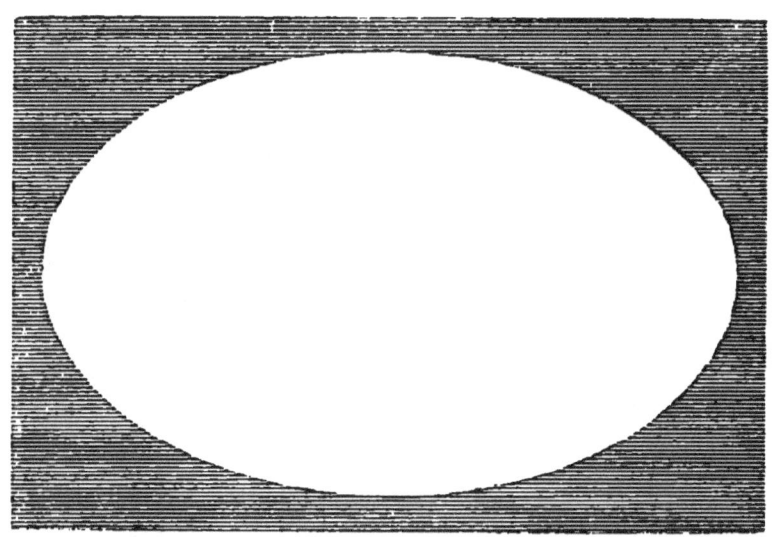

IMAGINARY PICTURE.

The Savans at the Bull's Eye passing upon the Doctor's poetry.

The poetry was submitted for revision and criticism to that same committee of most wonderful savans, who lodged in the very bull's eye of refinement, scholarly learning, and artistic culture, passed upon that grand translation by their most eminent brother savan of the "DIVINE COMMEDIA."

"By a love-sick chap,
   A poem writ, name Danté;
North of the heel tap,
   In boot-shape Itálee."

This matter was finally settled to the general satisfaction of the illuminatii, excepting on one point—Dr. Oliver Wendell Humes entered on record his solemn protest against

IMAGINARY PICTURE.
The Printers in Council passing upon the Doctor's punctuation.

his poetry being used as our author has handled it. He thought if a pump was started with his water, it ought to be jerked through upon it.

The punctuation was submitted to six delegates from the typographical unions of six of our principal cities, convened for the purpose. Alas, here was the most trouble of all! No two printers could agree upon a single point. One thought there ought to be a colon where was a semi-colon—another a dash where was a period—another a comma where *was* nothing, and so on interminably. At the close of five days of unintermitted labor, without getting a single disputed point settled, the Doctor in despair put a *full stop* to the business by snatching up his MSS. from the table, and rushing from the room: after which he sent each of the gentlemen a free ticket to return to his wife and babies by the first through lightning train—and they went at once with a big *dash* and many *exclamations* and *interjections* at the Doctor, for his sudden unceremonious departure from their midst.

Just before Doctor Wideawake left he brought into our office a quantity of frames. He wanted his readers to draw upon their imaginations while they perused, and as an inducement to do this he has generously supplied frames free of expense. If his readers comply with his desires, this work will be the subject of the most varied and copious illustrations of any extant.

IMAGINARY PICTURE.

Doctor Wideawake depositing his frames.

We referred early in our curve to a painful incident as having occurred when the Doctor was last in our establishment. The day was excessively rainy, and he had left his umbrella —a most valuable article, of French manufacture—leaning against our safe. Accidentally turning from his writing, he saw a cormorant just passing out of the door with this prized rain protector. An act of such an unheard-of and monstrous a character aroused Dr. Wide-

ODDS AND ENDS. 37

awake to frenzy, and he darted after him like a high-spirited bantam who finds a neighbor stealthily invading the sanctity of his domestic relations. His departure is symbolized below. It will be perceived the last thing shown is the *feather* end, which simply illustrates that the *fuss* had its proper accompaniment.

ODDS AND ENDS.

CHAPTER A.

In which are introduced some noted historical characters; as the United States Moses, All Gammon, Lemuel Gulliver, Sinbad the Sailor, Baron Munchhausen, the Wandering Jew, with anecdotes of the same never before published.

ALONGSIDE is *ex*hibited an *ex*act copy of an *ex*cellent portrait of an *ex*traordinary personage sometimes termed the "*Great Accidentosity*," from which it is inferred he was a relative of Sancho Panza. He it was who, in an *ex*treme *ex*igency, *ex*erted himself to *ex*tricate Noah after he *ex*ultingly made his *ex*alting *ex*it from the ark. In those venerated lineaments you behold the United States "Moses" with his head *off!*

And Carl Rosa played upon the violin, while Madame Parepa sang:

> On Pisgah's mount
> I'll take MY stand,
> And guide thee, SAMBO,
> To the promised land.

> Temperance and purity
> In MY example lies;
> Come and be like ME!—
> Noble, great, and wise!

That the original portrait is accurate we know, for we were so told by the artist who painted it from life on the day of the happenings, by a knot of ends here in these pages untied, and given by us as related by him.

A comprehensive name had this artist. It was ALL. He was thus named because he so closely resembled his father's family — the *Gammons*. ALL GAMMON, according to revelations to us, was on familiar terms with some noted characters, as Lemuel Gulliver, Baron Munchhausen, Sinbad the Sailor, the Wandering Jew, and Jack the Giant Killer.

Lemuel Gulliver was fond of the seaside, and a glorious good fellow on board a sailboat in a squall. His knack at making an appetizing chowder was unequaled.

Baron Munchausen ever exhibited a delicate regard for the truth. He was the real hero of the charming anecdote of the boy, cherry-tree, and hatchet, and that immortal expression, "Papa, I can't tell a lie," which we have seen related, although we may be mistaken, as an incident in the history of one G. Washington.

Sinbad the Sailor, early in life, run the smack "*Dragon,*" in the onion trade between Weathersfield and the Hook. At the age of twenty he followed oystering for a living. *And Carl Rosa played upon the violin, while Madame Parepa sang*:

> "It was a tall young oysterman,
>   Lived by the river side;"
> ·His Love a pewter snuff-box had,
>   And left him when she died.

After this afflicting dispensation, Sinbad commanded a stern-wheel boat in the Arkansas River trade. He was an especial favorite with the Underwriters, who paid him a large premium for the privilege of insurance. He was one of four brothers—Sin*bad*, Sin*worse*, Sin*more*, and Sin*less*. Sinworse was an officer of the Yazoo Tigers, in the Confederate army; Sinmore a Knight of the Golden Circle, and Past Grand of the Silver Triangle; while Sinless *walked in*, and then *trotted out* for woman's rights. All four were of irreproachable morals; that is, no one reproached them because of their possession.

The Wandering Jew was All Gammon's chum. He married for his 630th wife a young grass widow from an obscure town in Illinois, called, we believe, Chicago. She had been for some time browsing on dry feed.

IMAGINARY PICTURE.
Wedding of the Wandering Jew and the Chicago lady, who becomes his 630th wife.

The courtship was romantic. They exchanged photographs; their wedding tour was to Alaska; the sudden change of climate killed her—she *sweat* to death. The late Government Expedition, from a chaste design, erected a monument to her memory. The inscription is an honor to the American Union, and will live and shine a gem in *defunct* literature. The funeral ceremonies were impressive. A procession, preceded by a brass band blowing *wind* instruments, marched to the spot— sailors, soldiers, and marines; so some of the *marines told* All Gammon as it was told to them.

IMAGINARY PICTURE.

Funeral of the Jew's 630th wife.

That same evening the Wandering Jew proposed, for his 631st wife, to an Alaska maiden, whom he found feasting on blubber and train oil. She put the "*open* and *shut*" upon him; saucily laid one finger under her left eyelid, and pulled it down. This made her look wicked. Closing her eyelid, she next twitched a mitten from her hand, and threw at him in contempt. It was a fur mitten.

The Jew gave a howl of anguish, turned on his heel and ran rapidly northward for six days and seven nights, when, at dawn of the seventh day, he reached the North Pole. Having in past times taken a quarter's lessons in the art from Jack the Giant Killer, he began to climb, and by dusk had mounted to its top. When last seen he was a-sitting upon its apex, and with a woe-begone expression gazing into

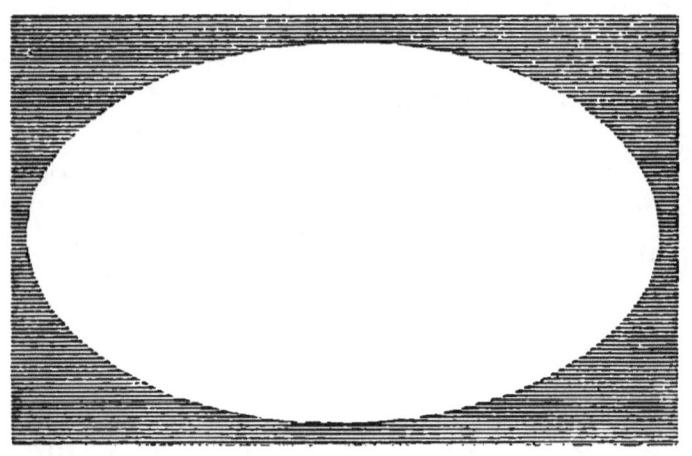

IMAGINARY PICTURE.

The Wandering Jew a-sitting on the North Pole.

vacancy, his shadow, in the low position of the luminary in that high altitude, reaching seventy miles. It was then broken short off by striking against an iceberg.

ODDS AND ENDS. 45

And Carl Rosa played upon the violin, while Madame Parepa sang:

O Alaska maid! O Alaska maid!
How could you serve me so?
I'm shivering on this northern pole,
And to it tight shall grow.

IMAGINARY PICTURE.

The Alaska maiden gives the Jew the mitten.

The Jew had been weeping, for long tear-formed icicles hung from his bearded jaws and glistened in the Arctic sun.

ODDS AND ENDS. 47

CHAPTER B.

Which describes how Mr. Noah was extricated from an unpleasant little happening by Andy, Secretaries Sewap and McKashlock, General Grent, Ben Botlaw, and others; the discovery of Chicago; auction of George Francis Fastline, and the jig of the strong-minded.

THE Noahs were ancestors of mine, but by my mother's side *only*. Mr. Noah's first name was Jonathan. He was of considerable stature, and corpulent; his visage rubicund and jolly.

On leaving the ark he was so jubilant that, unmindful of the saturated condition of the soil, he shouted, "Hurra for Andy Jinsin!" and then giving a circular swing, sprang off, sinking to his neck in the soft unctuosity. Some passengers going by in an omnibus stage bribed the driver with twenty cents in postal currency to stop. Among these were Billy Sewap, Jerry Darkname, and others, beside Andy Jinsin himself, who, with a shocking familiarity, they called to his face, "*Mose!*" They tried to pry Mr. Noah out with some rails from an old Virginia fence hard by. All in vain, until Secretary McKashlock applied the *financial screws*. The effect was marvelous. He came out at once with a pop and an effervescence.

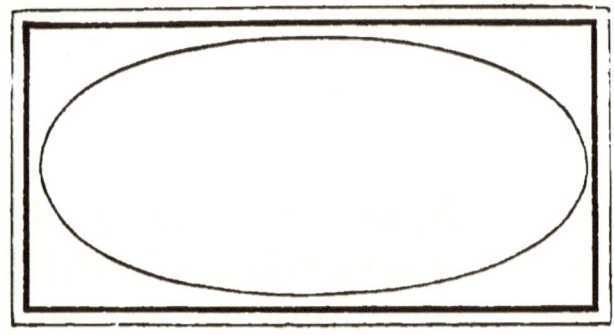

IMAGINARY PICTURE.

Secretary McKashlock extricates Mr. Noah by applying the financial screws.

General Grent, who had been outside with the driver smoking, bossed the job, during which he consumed several cigars—*eight* boxes of long nines, a present from Ben Walkonbottom, when the General had his horse talk.

And Carl Rosa played upon the violin, while Madame Parepa sang:

"And when he next doth ride abroad,
  May you and I be there to see,"
If mounted on a steed of gold,
  But not on *spavined currency.*

Mr. Noah was taken to Plymouth Rock to be cleaned, when Ben Botlaw hove in view, coming across the Hingham Meadows with his Woman's Order pinned across his breast, and over his back a coffee-bag, loaned by the Great American Tea Company. Staggering up, he threw down his burden with a puff and a grunt. As it was emptied, out came two bushels of marine shells,* from the Dutch

---

* We asked the author if he noticed that any *silver spoons* came out of that bag, upon which he fired up in great indignation, and tartly replied: "That was a vile, coppery slander; that old Ben down there was the rightest man in the rightest place that ever was seen; there never was such a perfect fit." He said "it wiped out all his old sins of commission before the big fuss came on, when he strutted in such *high feather* at the Convention of Salamanders, in the City of Game Cocks." We agreed with him.—*The Publisher.*

Gap Canal. When General Grent described to him the exhuming process, he said the old patriarch "came up like a cork out of a *bottle*," at which Ben's face suddenly dropped.

And Carl Rosa played upon the violin, while Madame Parepa sang:

> He was bottled tight,
> Was bottled long;
> 'T was on the Jeem's,
> So goes the song.
>
> 'T was there he fumed,
> 'T was there he fretted,
> 'T was there he sissed,
> And effervesced.

George Francis Fastline, assisted by two strong-minded, seized the shells and scraped Mr. Noah into a presentable condition, and then with modesty improved the occasion. He unrolled a map of his lots in Omaha to auction, while Theodore Tellem rung the *bell* and *cried* profusely. They were started at five millions a running foot, which, considering the currency, PENDLETUM'S WINDBACKS, Secretary McKashlock thought reasonable.

The size of the map was uncommon, extending so uply that the man in the moon and his wife were enabled, from the porch of their new gothic cottage, to seize and hold the upper corners to allow Fastline to spread. The lower

IMAGINARY PICTURE.

Old Ben Bollaw emptying the shells upon Plymouth Rock.

corners were held by two gas-bags from that obscure town in Illinois of which we have spoken—the name has slipped our memory. Oh! now we recollect! it is from a Nemonic

—*Crow*. It originated in a little private scrap of history.

Father Marquette, the French Jesuit missionary, in his early explorations came to a tad-pole sort of a spot near the southern end of the Lake, Michigan. The only inhabitant

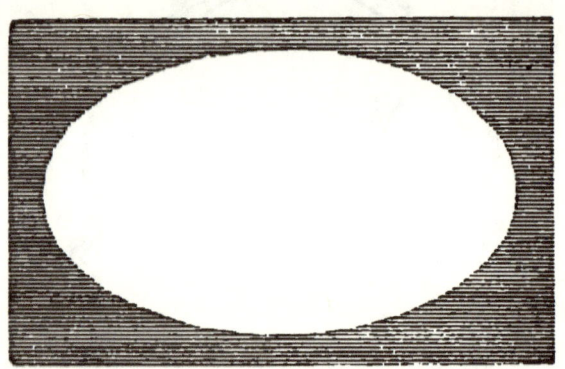

IMAGINARY PICTURE.

The discovery of Chicago. Father Marquette is frightened at the Crow, and the Crow at Father Marquette.

was a crow, a-sitting on her nest in the vicinity of a slough. Frightened—he being the first missionary she had ever seen—she gave a loud "*caw*," and then flew away.

At this moment the good father was, alone, cautiously making his way by stepping from bog to bog. He was so startled by the sudden uprising of the bird, and her loud, horrid cry, that he raised up his arms and sprang back in terror.

Alighting in a soft spot, he came near losing his life, for he at once went down like a stone in a mortar-bed, sinking up to his middle, and would have gone entirely under had he not caught hold of a stout bog, by which he was, after much difficulty, enabled to extricate himself. He was so thoroughly panic-stricken by his narrow escape, that he durst not again trust himself on his feet in such a treacherous locality. He lay flat on his bowels, and worked his way out in that position as best he could, by pulling himself from bog to bog, glad enough to escape even in that manner.

The incident made a profound impression on Father Marquette, and in giving the details to Roger Williams, after his banishment to Rhode Island, the venerable priest said, in his broken English, in alluding to the sudden uprising of the miserable bird, *"She caw, then go!"* hence the name. In our day, the place has quite a number of the genus "caw" known as "SHE CAW GEESE."

54 ODDS AND ENDS.

And Carl Rosa played upon the violin, while Madame Parepa sang:

> Birds of a feather
> Will flock together,
> Perch on slender legs,
> Coo, and lay their eggs.
>
> Some too strong for food,
> Yet others very good;
> The whole, indeed, quite small,
> And only eggs, after all!

IMAGINARY PICTURE.

The strong-minded dancing a jig to stow away the Pendletum windbacks in a coffee-bag of the Great American Tea Company.

The sale finished, the big bag of the Great American Tea Company was filled by the female assistants, and the cramming process finished by their alternately dancing a jig upon its open top. Wearing bloomers, their saltatory agility was such as to be suggestive of the "Black Crook."

And Carl Rosa played upon the violin, while Madame Parepa sang:

> In a world of woe and wrong,
>   We'll dance in reckless glee,
> We go in for POWER and PLACE,
>   And a fig for the CURRENCY!
> The fiends below do dance,
>   So merrily dance we.

ODDS AND ENDS. 57

CHAPTER C.

Which describes the Pendletum Currency; ascent of and bursting of the balloon; fall of the Unterrified and resuscitation of Jawge; swelling, bursting, and transmutation of Eight-Hour Sam into a thunder cloud.

THE Pendletum currency merits notice. We possess one hundred of the million-dollar bills. Still our great apprehension is the Alms-House. The face of the note has engraved upon it gas-works, bubbles, a kite, a bladder, wind instruments, as trumpets, trombones, tin horns, bassoons, and a pair of bellows. These devices are relieved by a dark-toned lathework, shown under the microscope to be a field of grass, suggestive for what it *concealed.*

And Carl Rosa played upon the violin, while Madame Parepa sang:

"He wriggled in and wriggled out,
 And tried to make the people doubt

> Whether the *snake* that made the track,
> Was going South, or coming back."

The vignette is an elegant work where Art delineates History. An ascending balloon is filled with a delegation, all of the Unterrified, excepting Eight-Hour Sam—alas! poor Tray! Luminously shines there the smiling visage of Jawge himself. All are attired as harlequins, and with fool's caps. A jolly crowd are upward gazing. These people also wear fool's caps, and it is said their fore pieces were sheep's pelts. Above the balloon the Confederate flag is flaunting.

And Carl Rosa played upon the violin, while Madame Parepa sang:

> Up with stripes and bars, boys!
>   We'll give the Blue Backs Jesse!
> Give the Blue Backs Jesse, boys,
>   With our NEW REBEL tune.

The back of the bill is a continuation of the History. Art there perpetuates the culminating event, the collapse and fall of the Unterrified. Some were killed outright: some fell into a swamp: some into tree tops, and were saved. Jawge tumbled head first souse into an ancient tan vat. When they saw him *fall* all felt he had gone *up*. He was fished out by the Humane Society, who did every thing

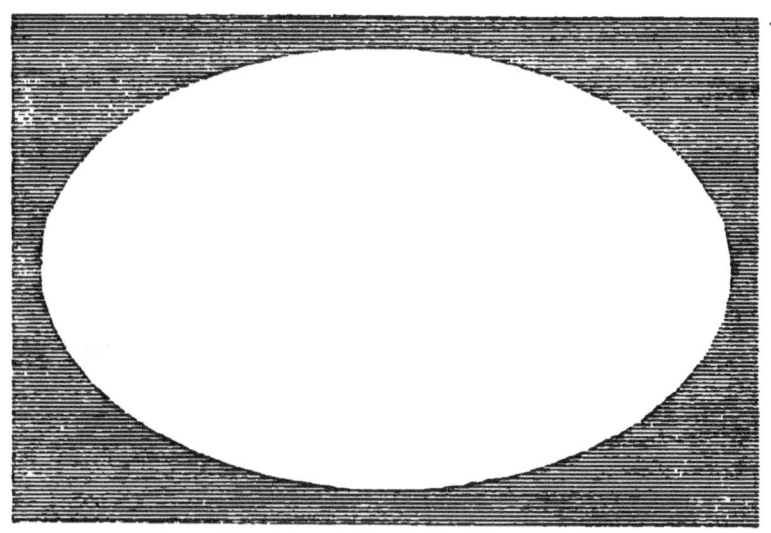

IMAGINARY PICTURE.

Collapse of the balloon, and fall of the Unterrified, and Screeching.

for his resuscitation. He was rolled in a barrel. He was held up by the legs to empty out the tan liquid. All in vain, when rosy-cheeked, good-humored Aleck Longman came up and administered three bags of nitrous oxygen. At the second Jawge sneezed twice and kicked. At the third he was restored to the bosom of his family, and the embraces of the Unwashed and Screeching.

And Carl Rosa played upon the violin, while Madame Parepa sang:

> "Oh! ye ragged throng of dimmocrats,
>   As thick as rats;
>   Moll Cary's come to town
>   To dance with Deacon Ives."

This is not all the history, nor all the picture. Five miles high in air, at the point of collapse, was a solitary figure. This was Eight-Hour Sam—immortal Sam. Unable to descend, too etherial to do so, he was at his normal position in the sky.

When this event occurred, the astronomer at the Washington Observatory had his telescope bearing upon the point. To a deputation of Eight-Hour men inquiring for the facts in the apotheosis of their champion, he stated that Sam soon engaged in a series of gyrations, as if making a financial speech in the high tide line, which he doubtless was, and illustrated, too, by rhetorical flourishes from his old temperance orations, when he figured so usefully in the regimentals of the cold-water army. His face was southward. He walked too and fro; gesticulated severely; stamped; cast up his arms; dove his hands through his hair, and shook his black, massive locks, as a lion shaketh his mane. Sam was evidently on a tare—was at his loftiest flight.

And Carl Rosa played upon the violin, while Madame Parepa sang:

> "Old King Cole was a jolly old soul,
> He had his fiddlers three;"
> And he *play'd* IN and they *play'd* OUT,
> 'T was all about the CURRENCY.

At the end of an hour, Sam accidentally turned northward, when he started as in wonder. From his elevation he had made a discovery—descried the melancholy figure of the Wandering Jew seated upon the apex of the North Pole. His soul was touched with compassion: and he went through the pantomime of love and courtship, during the address he made to the heart-broken man. He was probably advising the Jew to leave his roosting-place among the icebergs and eternal snows, and come South, and propose for his 631st wife to one of the Fox girls. What the effect was upon the Jew is unknown. As he was not then heard from, it is supposed he was so tightly frozen to the pole, that he could not go a courting without an *unpropitious* rending of his garments.

And Carl Rosa played upon the violin, while Madame Parepa sang:

> "Oh! woman, in our hours of ease,
> Uncertain, coy, and hard to please;"
> When short of FUNDS, in thee a change we see,
> A PURRing Angel RUBS for *Currency!*

After this, at 4 o'clock P. M., a surprising phenomena ensued:—seen by the Sons of Women and Daughters of Men below. To the horror of the Eight-Hour advocates, Sam's body began to expand. The ether in him, relieved by his altitude from its usual atmospheric pressure, had unrestrained action. Every thing swelled in its natural proportion, head, arms, legs, body, and all his features. Each *particular hair* on his head arose on end and expanded also. In ten minutes he had

ODDS AND ENDS. 63

swollen out one hundred feet—in ten more had attained a thousand—in a third ten to five thousand! His eyes were upturned, and the whole expression was of rhapsody. A nimbus

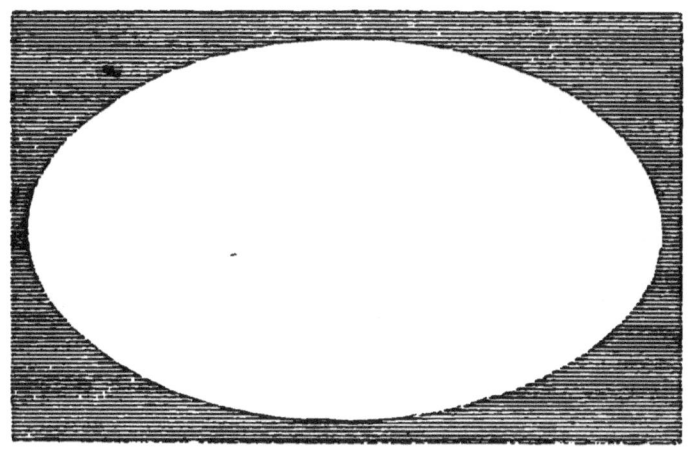

IMAGINARY PICTURE.

Sam in the sky, just before he burst, swollen to a mile in dimensions.

or halo, as of glory, seemed as it were to envelop and emanate from that immense presence!

What an object! a man in the sky with a body a mile long, and eyes larger than a meeting-house! What couldn't such eyes see?

And Carl Rosa played upon the violin, while Madame Parepa sang:

> "Such folks as ME are very rare,
> And few and far between;"
> Small birds are often seen in air,
> But rare, have blad——

At this point, Carl broke his fiddle-string, and Madame was seized with a fit of coughing, so the verse was unfinished. Carl turned over his violin, unlocked a little recess in its under side, and taking therefrom one of Brown's bronchial troches, with a smile and bow passed it to Madame. In a few moments they were again ready.

And Carl Rosa played upon the violin, while Madame Parepa sang:

> "Oh! would n't I like to catch him,
> Whoever he may be!
> Would n't I give him particular fits,
> The chap that looks like me!"

Another phenomena ensued. A loud report, simultaneous with a tornado-like gust, came from above, and before any could take in its meaning, prostrated every man, woman, and child in that crowd. Gold in Wall St. tumbled down to par, crushing all the *Bears.* The Board adjourned, and the crowd lay senseless: not a soul even kicked.

On the recovery of the people from their horizontal posture, a vast, round, bulging, wool-like cloud was resting over the spot. The rest of the sky was one ocean of blue. The cloud looked beautifully in the sunlight of that summer afternoon, soft and serene, as if inviting to repose. It floated tranquilly to the west; was lit up grandly by the declining sun in crimson and gold, changed into a deep purple, and then became dark and ominous. At intervals, from low in the horizon darted flashes of lightning, mingled with sullen rumblings as of distant thunder. Finally all disappeared, and night and silence was in the Heavens.

It was the last seen of well-meaning Eight-Hour Sam!

He had attained his Nirwena!

Had been absorbed in the Great Essence!

Poor Sam! If ever he again perchance to visit our Earth, it will be in the form of much wind, considerable cold water, and pockets full of spavined currency.

And Carl Rosa played upon the violin, while Madame Parepa sang:

> And the waters do roll,
> And the wind doth blow,
> On the large lake of Ohio.

That day was one to be remembered. The bar at Delmonico's was never before so beset by despondent bears: and when the people went home at night they had something to think of and to talk about.

CHAPTER D.

Which tells of the discovery of Mr. Noah's boots in the Rocky Mountains by laborers on the Pacific Railroad, and gives some anecdotes of the Noahs, which shows they were much like our sort of folks.

JONATHAN NOAH, Esq., met with a loss by his exhilarating jump. The mud had boot-jacked him out of a pair of new cowhides that Adams' Express had dead-headed through from the Land of Nod. They were a Christmas present from the Noddies. Those identical boots were found a short time since by some laborers in the Rocky Mountains while excavating for the Pacific Railroad. They appeared as was natural after having worked their way through from the other side—*singed* from the internal heats, and, of course, *bottoms up*.

We are pleased to speak respectfully of Mr. Noah's sons. Japheth was a solemn-looking young man, with a mysterious air. He had on a Freemason's apron. Ham was pig-eyed, and his hair and beard like bristles. He used freely Hall's Sicilian Hair Renovator. Shem was a simpering, flippant youth, who wore a

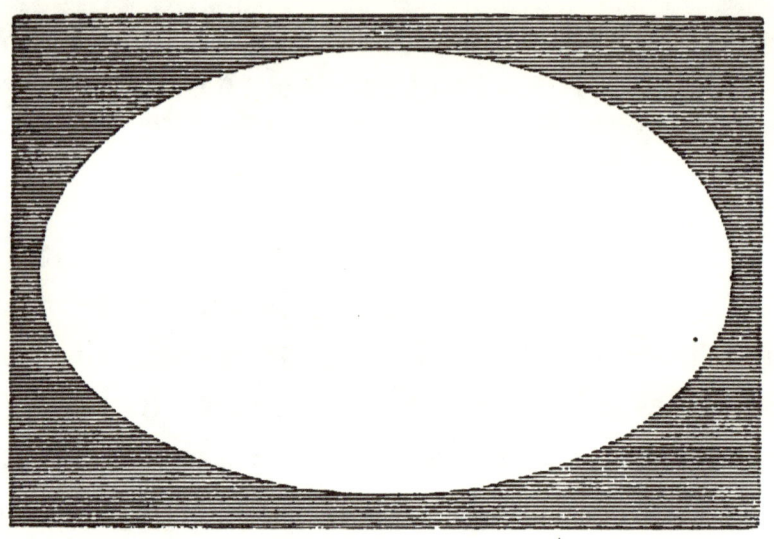

IMAGINARY PICTURE.

Discovery of Noah's boots by laborers on the Pacific Railroad in the Rocky Mountains. They appeared as was natural after having come through from the other side—considerably singed from the internal heats, and bottoms up.

bob-tailed coat, a low, top-heavy hat, and lisped. He "tho't thar had bin a conthidable of a thower." He thought right.

Mr. Noah's three grown daughters—for it seems he *had* girls, also—were substantial, home-bred bodies, at no dangerous elevation in the sciences, but well trained in housewifery. Although themselves good enough for "human nature's daily food," they had taken a course in the culinary art from Professor Blow. They had never been "abroad;" indeed, had not been out of Asia. Pleasant excursions to the Land of Nod comprised the extent of their travels. Unfamiliar with any language but their own, they wisely judged it better to talk good sense and correct grammar in that one than folly and bad grammar in a dozen. Upon the good earth where they dwelt, in those far-away worlds they saw glittering above, they found ample sources for the expansion of their intellects and the gratification of their tastes, without losing their fresh, young, beautiful years in the mysteries of the linguistic symbols of strange peoples.

They were, however, human beings; girls usually are; therefore they had a weakness—*trails*. These were thirty yards long. They carried respectively in their hands the latest issues of Godey's Lady's Book, Madam

Demorest's Magazine of Fashions, and Harper's Bazaar.

Their wardrobes were brought ashore by the elephant, in his trunk; their Wheeler and Wilson's, on his back. With all their good sense, it thus seems they partook of some of the vanities of this strange world, of which the greatest can fathom so little.

And Carl Rosa played upon the violin, while Madame Parepa sang:

OUR LIFE OUTLINED.

'T is a queer ball,
    Where we jog on our "pins;"
We can't jump away,
    And see how it spins.

'T is here we are born,
    Play, work, laugh, and sigh,
Love, wed, have children,
    Grow old, and then die.

Still round the ball whirls,
    And we are forgot,
None care and none know—
    Oblivion's our lot.

The names of these young damsels were Polly Ann, Sally Jane, and Hephzibah.

Mrs. Noah was a match for her spouse in stature, corpulence, and exuberance. The long spell of damp weather had deepened her naturally roseate hue. Ancient expressions enlivened her conversation; as,

"*O, my!*"
"*I want to know!*"
"*You don't say so!*"
"*I never!*"
"*Do tell!*"
"*Law, Suz!*" etc.

She possessed that rare combination of being both a good listener and a good talker. Often have we seen the old lady, in one of her social moods, at work in her easy chair, with her heavy silver spectacles on, her stocking-basket by her side, in which, maybe, puss had crawled, and lay curled.

Such was her talent for mimicry, so well could she light up the salient points of a ludicrous story, that, if it had been ordained that death was to come to us from laughter, long ere this we should have been screwed up in a box. Luckily, nothing worse ever befell us than to tumble from our chair, which happened on three separate occasions, as we well remember. No richer treat existed than to hear Mrs. Noah *talk* when she *darned*.

Whenever any excitable person annoyed her listeners in an officious zeal to help her out in any story she was relating, by interpolating an unimportant item, she had a peculiar way of brushing them aside. Lifting up her arm, with her index finger pointing from her clasped hand, she brought down that member with the emphasis of a pump-handle, at the same time looking the offender sternly in the face, and exclaiming in an imperious tone, *"Don't interrupt!"*

IMAGINARY PICTURE.

Portrait of Mrs. Noah as she looked when relating some of her funny stories.

It was the only unamiable thing in her character, which our regard for the truth compels us to notice, though we are sorry for it; but then she was touched on a tender point—felt her reputation at stake.

To know a genial old lady like her, who

had grown wisely with her years, sipping sweets by the way instead of acids, was worth a luscious plum. She wanted her "gals" to enjoy themselves as she had done. They had no secrets from her, and she entered into their little plans with a zest that kept her heart fresh and young as spring-time. Instead of lamenting modern fashions, she only laughed at them, and no more expected old heads on young shoulders than the full moon in the time of horns.

She had brought up her children well, and now, as they were mostly grown, had her reward. They had been sent regularly to church and Sabbath-school, and were not allowed to play out on the holy day until after sunset. It is true, they sometimes did this, but it was only toward evening when a deceiving cloud obscured the luminary, by which interposition of Nature the little ones innocently gained the trifling matter of half an hour or so. It was never laid up or registered anywhere against them, we verily believe. Don't understand us they were *perfect* children; by no means. They had their little faults, and they were so clearly their own that none disputed their title. Sometimes they quarreled with each other; and they even had been known, "*Sabba'*-day" afternoons, when the old folks

IMAGINARY PICTURE.

The Noah children playing in the garden "Sabba'-day." Catching bumble-bees off the hollyhawks with clam-shells, and then holding 'em up to their ears to hear 'em sing!

were a-napping in their chairs, to slyly steal out the back door into the "gardin'," pick currants and green apples, and eat 'em; or catch bumble-bees from off the hollyhawks between two clam-shells, and having got 'em thus imprisoned, hold 'em up to their ears to hear 'em sing!

But if they had not occasionally been naughty, they never would have "repented," and this would have been "agin natur," you know. They were made to read the Bible, in course, yet were allowed to skip the "begats."

System prevailed in the household, and just enough restraint for the good of all. In general, we may say, it was always sunshine there, excepting, of course, during the period of the great flood.

Some of the neighbors who did n't go to their "meeting," but went to what they called "*the* church," said the Noahs were "*blue*."

This was true, but it was with Heaven's own blue, which does so swell the soul on any fair day, when one happens to cast his eyes above, and get glimpses of it, maybe through the fresh tender leaves of the wood, while the melody of sweet singing birds fills the air.

We must give some anecdotes of the Noahs. Japheth, the oldest son, notwithstanding his grave expression of countenance, possessed an overweening love of fun, united to unusual simplicity of character. When he was a boy, he believed every thing that was told him; and this credulity, this honesty of soul sometimes rendered him a butt for older lads.

IMAGINARY PICTURE.

How Mr. Noah looked when he saw Japheth's Water-Proof Hat after it went a-swimming.

When about six years of age, he left his home with others, one Saturday afternoon in early summer, to bathe at a beautiful spot about two miles distant, where a clear stream of fresh water wound through green meadows, inclosed by soft wooded hills.

That day his father had bought him a new, white hat, with the promise of a fine pocket-knife, if he would preserve it in good "go-to-meeting" order for a certain space of time. Japheth said he would "try.".

This hat he proudly wore on this occasion. On the way thither, a large, rollicking lad snatched it from his head with the exclamation of "Ho! Japheth, where did you get so much new hat?" Then looking inside he read in large gilt letters, "WATER-PROOF!" "Ho! water-proof, is it!" he continued, "Japheth, put this hat in the water, it won't hurt it!"

The little, simple boy believed him. He was at that tender age when he thought that the blue hills he saw from his father's home bounded the whole world.

The trusting, simple faith of young souls just opening to the impressions of this existence is always so beautifully touching that the hearts of the good every-where respond in sympathy. There never was a thoroughly good person that did not love children.

In full belief that no harm would ensue, Japheth soaked the hat in the water, using it as freely as if it had been a dipper. Of course, it was ruined, "an awful object" to behold. Its flat, stiff, circular top was changed into an irregular hemisphere, while its rim hung down limpsy as the ears of a poodle puppy. Japheth said he could not forget, if he lived to be old as Methuselah, the heart-broken expression of his father when he saw that hat on his return home on that Saturday evening. As a punishment, he was tied to the bedpost the next day, while the family were at "meeting."

Many years later, one bland, delicious, dreamy-like morning in spring, Japheth was seated on the rear porch of the old homestead. Before him lay the garden and orchard in their fresh vegetation, just bursting into life. Here and there a bonfire, with its crackling flame and ascending smoke, was consuming the withered vegetation of the by-gone year, while the warm sun, drinking up the rising moisture from the earth, gave to the air a peculiar, tremulous, wavy motion. If one did n't know, one might fancy that Nature was "on a high"—had taken "a wee drop too much!" It had, but it was, a good temperance beverage—*water!*

Japheth was enjoying the scene to the full, when an impending event, casting its shadow before, aroused in him the sense of the ludicrous. In great glee, he summoned his mother, and the rest of the family, from the adjoining room, where they were having a pleasant chat around the table, at the close of the morning meal, for mirth, even more than misery, likes company.

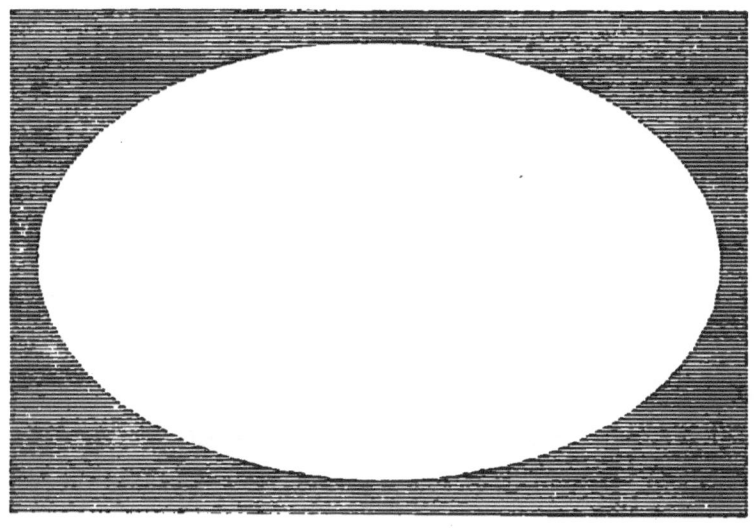

IMAGINARY PICTURE.

Mr. Noah's little mishap in the garden.

Some twenty rods distant, their hired man was up in an apple-tree, sawing off a branch, while Father Noah was standing on the ground, lending his assistance. He had grasped the end of it with both hands, and was pulling back with the entire weight of his body. The old gentleman was attired in slippers, a black stove-pipe hat, and a loose, red morning gown.

The attitude in which he had placed himself formed a right-angled triangle, the upright being the loose gown as it hung from his shoulders, his body the hypotenuse, and the ground beneath the base.

When all had fairly gathered, and were looking on in merry suspense, the catastrophe came—the sudden breaking of the branch, causing a sudden destruction of the triangle, and the prostration of Father Noah flat on his back on the Earth. None of the family suffered from indigestion on that day.

A more ludicrous scene occurred to Mother Noah. One evening, at a masquerade party, she was unexpectedly called to her home, and on leaving the ladies' dressing-room, she resolved to slip out unobserved, by a back stairway which she supposed led out of doors. This was an error, for the door, at its foot, opened into the gentlemen's dressing-room; and at this identical moment some six or eight of them, not in a parlor costume condition, were there changing their attire for the masquerade.

Mother Noah had no sooner placed her-

ODDS AND ENDS. 81

self in position to descend than her feet slipped, and she glided down those stairs on her back like a heavy plank, struck the door with her feet with the force of a battering ram,

IMAGINARY PICTURE.

Mrs. Noah's little mishap at the Masquerade.

when it flew open with great noise, and she slid into the center of the room. The gentlemen, in panic at this sudden apparition of an immense old lady, fled under and behind the bed and in the closet. Hose-covered limbs in vanishing movements met her eyes as she thus lay flat on her back. It was quite an event.

We should not relate such trivial incidents as these, were it not that any facts, however slight, connected with the world-wide known family who lived in the Ark, through the great flood, will always be read with an unwonted relish. Besides, they have a philosophical use—illustrate the important fact that thousands of years ago people were very much as they are now.

CHAPTER E.

Which tells of the flattering invitation Mrs. Noah receives from Mr. Stewat to go through his dry goods establishment by railroad; also introduces young Harry Wood Beachem, a journeyman preacher, and author of Blue-covered Literature.

WHILE Mrs. Noah was leaving the Ark, Aleck Stewat, a young dry goods dealer, came aboard and told her he should regard it as an honor if she would allow him to show her through his establishment and see his new styles; he had some splendid bargains in poplins. She would, on entering his door, find a train of cars and a locomotive ready, and as it was only forty miles around, she could soon do it up.

And Carl Rosa played upon the violin, while Madame Parepa sang:

"Singing through the forests,
Rattling over ridges,
Shooting under arches,
Rumbling over bridges;

ODDS AND ENDS.

> Whizzing through the mountain,
> Buzzing o'er the vale—
> Bless me! this is pleasant,
> Riding on the rail!"

IMAGINARY PICTURE.

Internal view of Stewat's Dry Goods Store. Railroad train ready to take customers around.

Dry goods had charms, for she was a woman, and her eyes twinkled under the descriptions of the smooth-talking trader; but she had seen much in the newspapers lately of railroad accidents, and was too timid to venture. Had she known of the Accidency Insurance plan, the United Universe and the parts lying adjacent thereunto could not have stopped her. Fortunate ignorance for Mr. Noah's bank balance!

When this motherly soul came ashore, it was with an eye to population. She carried on each arm a new-born infant, and was smoking a charcoal pipe. We think this a modern invention; that was proof to the contrary, and here is more proof.

And Carl Rosa played upon the violin while Madame Parepa chanted:

> "The thing that hath been is,
> And that which shall be,
> And that which is done,
> Is that which shall be done,
> And there is no *new* thing under the sun."

No, not even "Odds and Ends!" Indeed, we have a vague impression that, in a world we lived in before we got here, we once made a book exactly like this. We repeat, the impression is *vague;* it is so much so that we should have *conscientious* scruples in swearing to the fact before a court of justice, and we hope we shall not be called upon.

On her arrival on *terra firma*, Mrs. Noah was met by Harry Wood Beachem, a young man, an itinerant lecturer, and peddler of blue-covered literature, which he carried in a knapsack on his back. He was designing to ultimately enter the ministry, and to furnish the means to obtain an education, had written and published several novels, which he was selling about from house to house.

His little brochures went by the term of BLUE-COVERED LITERATURE, simply because, under the guise of fiction, his tales contained sermons ingeniously worked in, and in such an attractive manner that, when one began to read, they went through them attentively from the beginning to the end without getting asleep over them, as they would have done had the preachment been given in the ordinary manner.

The idea of preaching in a novel shocked some delicate sensibilities. A sermon, to be to the point, should be divided into a certain number of heads, delivered in a regular, systematic manner, so that when the tenthly was reached, it would have its full *somnolent* effect.

Harry Wood Beachem was an universal favorite with the old farmers and their families throughout the country. In Noah's time, as well as in ours, none but persons in the decline of life engaged in agriculture; hence the propriety of the universal expression, "*old* farmers." He was so genial, so cheerful, so abounding in happy views of life, of men and things, that his presence shed universal sunshine. He thought that religion had been prevented from taking its full effect because its advocates had too generally presented its truths with elongated countenances and in wailing tones. As the living in conformity with the higher law was the greatest of all topics, he felt as though its advocacy was thus weakened by its continual presentation in lugubrious aspects.

His heart was so overflowing with kindly feeling that no room was left for enmity. If he should, on going through the forests, be bitten by a copperhead or any other venomous thing, almost his first emotion would be of sympathy for his enemy, on the supposition that it had acted under an error in supposing that he designed its injury; as an error when honestly held is truth to the person or thing holding it, he would thus respect the motive and forgive the offender.

At this time he had been delivering lectures to the farmers throughout that region, using for that purpose the district school-houses, to which the people repaired evenings, each family carrying with them one or more dipped candles to light up with.

IMAGINARY PICTURE.

Harry Wood Beachem lecturing to the old farmers in the "deestrict" school-house.

There was some talk of settling him where he had finished his theological course, over a congregation in that vicinity. The old farmers thought they could pay him a salary of about three hundred dollars. This, with an ample supply of potatoes, an annual *donation visit*, and abundance of *swamp oak* for fuel, certainly were brilliant

:nts for a young man at his start in

CHAPTER F.

Which gives an account of the meeting of young Harry Wood Beachem and Jawge H. Pendletum with Mrs. Noah, as she came out of the Ark, and the arrival of Wendell Feelups, Agagasay, Mr. Van Winkle, Max Marattlezak, and the Companies of " Mutual Friends," " Odd Friends," "Ye Gods and Little Fishes," "Uncle Sam's Men," "Ye Dickings Squad," ending with music from the Mewonica.

SOME natures are so joyous, so exuberant, so electric with life that this world seems to them a Heaven. Health bounds through their veins, benevolence expands their hearts, and gratitude to the Eternal fills their souls for having placed them on this wonderful revolving ball, that guided by his mysterious power goes whirling through the infinite regions of space in majestic grandeur and sublimity.

Even the smallest things minister to their sense of the beautiful. A ray of sunlight falls through the half-closed shutter, and the motes of floating dust are lit up in specks of glittering gold, and they are pleased.

Cultivating this sense, they find more and more to observe and enjoy, so that, as life advances, the fountain of delights continually expands, its waters become purer and deeper, and give more and more exquisite reflections of sky, mountain, foliage, and flowers. Why should they not love the world? It is their Maker's creature!

Sometimes people of this disposition become so exhilarated with joy, that they scarcely can contain themselves within those bounds of dignity becoming a race so wise, so wonderful as *us* human beings. With an irresistible desire to give vent to their exuberance they run! they jump! they shout! they laugh! they turn somersets, and roll in the grass like young colts let loose in green pastures.

Staid people—especially if their digestive apparatus is disordered—look on, and are shocked. Raising their hands in astonishment, they exclaim, "Why! they are *be-side* themselves!" So far from this being true they are simply themselves *alone* acting out their natures; and if they did n't draw the cork occasionally, and effervesce, would suffer from internal fermentation, although they might gain in external consideration.

Why such queer folks were ever created is an enigma that puzzles our philosophy to solve: but being once made, we can not much blame them for wanting to continue to live: and from motives of humanity we should allow them to do so. Still, we do honestly think it would be a public benefit, if they could be strangled at birth. It is too serious a world to have such goings on permitted!

Young Harry Wood Beachem was so happy, so overflowing with life, that it injured his influence as a preacher, especially with that serious-minded class, described so fully in the 23d chapter of Matthew.

On the morning he met Mrs. Noah coming out of the Ark, he had been walking through the woods, and beside the little, clear, babbling brooks, and was so exhilarated by the influences of Nature in her smiling mood, that he could n't well restrain himself from doing something ridiculous. Besides he had a keen appetite, and wanted his breakfast.

Giving the old lady a hearty slap between the shoulders, he inquired if she had any good home-made mince pie aboard, and some old

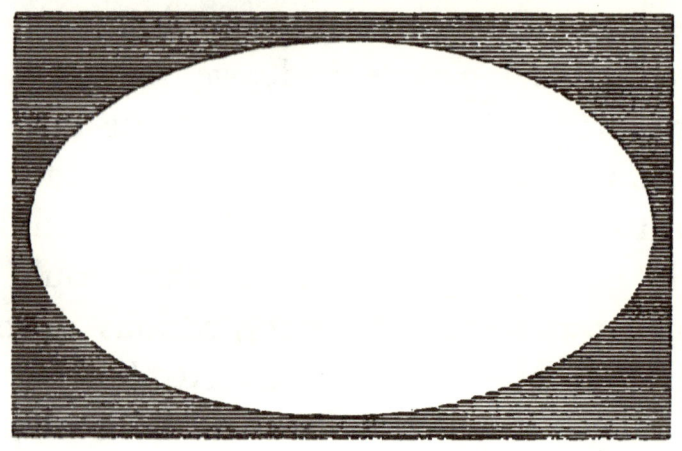

IMAGINARY PICTURE.

Mrs. Noah reads, while Harry Wood Beachem and Jawge H. Pendletum coddle the infants.

Goshen cheese; he wanted a snack, was almost starved, and while she was about it he shouldn't *object* to her drawing him a mug of cider to wash it down. She resented his mistaken familiarity in a dudgeon that was not so high, but that he appeased her by a present of a beautiful bouquet of freshly-plucked wild flowers, and a copy of his last issue: "Low Wood, or Rural Life in Bramble Land." Upon this Jawge H. Pendletum gave her an illustrated copy of his celebrated oration, "The Farmer Republic." Delighted with these attentions she passed to each of those gentlemen an infant, and they proceeded to coddle, while she proceeded to read.

And Carl Rosa played upon the violin, while Madame Parepa sang:

"Rock a bye, baby,
On the tree top,
When the wind blows,
The cradle will rock."

Mrs. Noah gave little low grunts of pleasure as she perused. Pausing for a moment to signify her appreciating sense of their genius, she took from a basket a snow-white napkin, unrolled it, and gave therefrom to each a freshly boiled doughnut, and a cold sausage. As for those doughnuts, the good old lady made them herself, and they were "just right." The sausages, too, were home-made, and could be eaten with that simple, trusting confidence, always so beautiful to behold.

Mr. Noah raised his *own* pork, and nobody else's. He had a neat inclosure at the end of his garden, where he boarded two or three intelligent creatures. It was his custom when he came home to his own dinner, to go out and first give them theirs. They knew his footsteps, and always greeted his coming with joyous demonstrations. Many a nice, tender, succulent ear of corn, plucked fresh on the spot, was received at his hands, and eaten with the relish of full health and a sound digestion. Then the old gentleman, who had a sort of weakness in wishing to make every thing about him happy, often took a chip, and rubbed their backs until they laid down and uttered in little short puffs, notes of joy, as though they were in Elysium.

> "Where ignorance is bliss,
> 'T is folly to be wise,"

is an applying quotation you may have seen before! If so, it won't hurt you to see it once more before you die. And the blissful ignorance of Father Noah's boarders consisted in the fact that they knew nothing of the frosts of November, that season termed "killing time," when the departure of the spirits of piggies to that land where the spirits of piggies go, finds a requiem in falling leaves, and wailing winds, and somber skies.

IMAGINARY PICTURE.

Father Noah's Boarders receiving at his hands benevolent ministrations.

When Mother Noah so kindly extended her hospitality to those gentlemen, the infants had their eyes open. They started up at once and made a *grab* for the cakes. The result was uncertain, when a hyena-like yell announced the arrival of, who do you think? Nobody else but WENDELL FEELUPS, and *all* there was of him had come—nothing was left behind!

And Carl Rosa played upon the violin, while Madame Parepa sang:

"Come, little boy Blue,
  And blow up your horn;
  The sheep's in the meadow,
  The cow's in the corn!"

Mounting a stump, Wendell entered upon a general cussing. He cussed the Earth—cussed the Heavens above the Earth—cussed the Waters under the Earth—cussed all that therein was, that walked, or flew, or swam—cussed all that therein was, that did n't walk, nor fly, nor swim—cussed the Past, the Present, and the Future—cussed what never was, what was not, and what never would be.

And Carl Rosa played upon the violin, while Madame Parepa sang:

"There was a man in our town,
  And he was wondrous wise;"
Said 't was so:—*knew it all*,
  And could n't but ADVISE!

Wendell was proceeding to cuss some other things, when a sharp blow was given by a hammer in the hands of AGAGASAY, a geological personage, on Plymouth Rock. The Earth quaked, the rock split, a cloud of vapor issued therefrom, when, lo! out from its midst arose an ancient man, with a long, white beard, reaching to his knees, bearing a rusty gun, and a dog as old and queer-looking as himself, by his side. He was a pre-Adamite—had been buried a million of years.

The people gathered around and inquired, "*Who are you?*" He mildly replied in a voice, tremulous with centuries, that he was a VAN WINKLE. The historians had erred in giving only the *initial letter* of his first name for his full name. The alphabet of the pre-Adamites had thirty letters, the last of which was the letter referred to—the *letter* RIP!

He thereupon handed out a card with his name engraved in full. To save a perpetuation of the error, we present a fac-simile. We

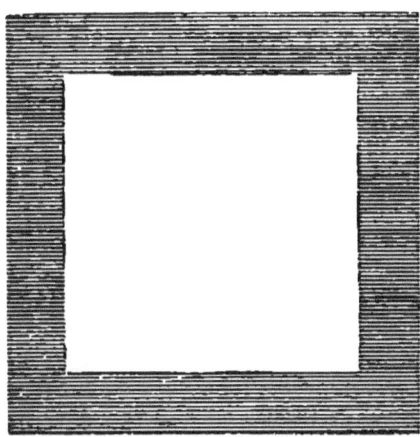

IMAGINARY PICTURE.

Agagasay having stricken Plymouth Rock with his hammer, Mr. Van Winkle and his dog appears. He has been buried a million of years.

hope posterity will be grateful to us. Our

> RIPSTIWIZEN VAN WINKLE, Esq.
>
> HIS CARD.

modest ambition is filled by association with memorable things.

And Carl Rosa played upon the violin, while Madame Parepa sang:

>   Some by their own light
>   Like punk do shine,
>   While I, poor soul,
>   Must borrow mine.

The Wood Beachem took notes of these revelations, for a literary project, when the strains of strange music turned all eyes, and stretched all necks to discover its source, as over the hill came dashing an enormous menagerie-like wagon, drawn by twelve white horses, and MAX MARATTLEZAK driving. With a crack of his whip, he circled into their midst, and then pulling back tautly on the lines, hallo'd *"Whoa!"*

Following Max was a procession on foot in two's, with linked arms. Each as they passed dropped their cards into the outspread apron of Mrs. Noah. All smiles at their attention, she exclaimed, "Gentlemen, I'm happy to see you. You will ever find my latch-string externally pendant."

And Carl Rosa played upon the violin, while Madame Parepa sang:

YANKEE HOSPITALITY.

Betty, run to the door,
   Show "them" people in!
Set chairs, sweep the hearth,
   Make things neat as a pin.

Oh, 't is you! so glad you've come!
   How's Aunt Keziah and Cousin Liz,
And baby, and all the folks "to hum,"
   And how's Grandpa's rheumatiz?

Betty, run, and some cider draw,
   Bring pie and cheese from off the rack!
Pray, move up, friends, and take a bite,
   And refresh with a little snack!

The first couple were Admiral Sammies and Gideon Wulles. The Admiral had come to open a shop for the sale of woman's duds, the captured clothing of the wives of officers of merchant vessels—fruits of his prowess on the high seas; the respectable Grandmamma to make new studies in naval architecture from Mr. Noah's model.

Succeeding these, arm in arm, talking lovingly together, and bearing knapsacks with the words as below given, were

1st Comp'y.

MUTUAL

FRIENDS.

Fitz John Purter & John Popa.
Jerry Darkname & Thaddeus Stingem.
Parson Brownhigh & General Lea.
Oliver Merton & Beriah Magorem.

Fernandy Would & Hunnycut.
Henry Clay Deam & Dick Yites.
Commodore Vanderconstruct & Ledger Bonny.
Thurlow Badplant & Horace Agreele.

Ralph Waldo Emmerem & James Gordon Bennem.
Brick Pummice & Oliver Wendell Humes.
Sootant D. Booregard & John Foreneigh.
George B. Macklenum & Hannibell Hamlan.
Mayor Moonrow & John C. Freehighhill.
Goruner Seymuch & Secretary Stunem.
Mylord Feelmore & Wm. Floyd Garrisome.
Theodore Tellem & Wm. Gilmore Sammies.

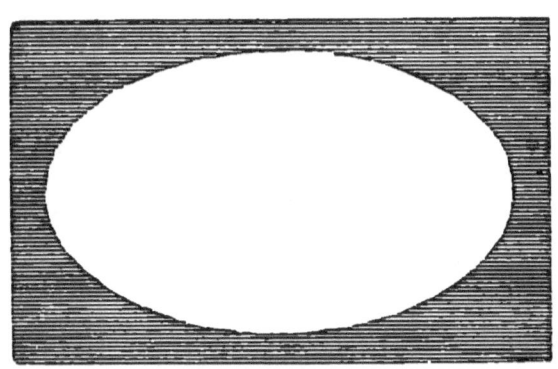

IMAGINARY PICTURE.

Perspective view of the Grand Procession.

Next succeeded an extraordinary body of individuals, mostly in twos, not with linked arms, but arranged opposite each other, pulling by a drag rope a huge grindstone mounted on wheels. They also bore knapsacks lettered as here shown. Attired in the costumes of their respective times, stations, and nationalities, they might, without an unpardonable exaggeration, be termed a somewhat mixed assemblage.

They were in the order here given; the first named in each couplet having hold of the rope by the right hand, the last named by the left hand.

> 2D COMP'Y.
>
> ODD
>
> FRIENDS.

Sancho Panza & Benedict Arnold were the leading couplet.

Then came Peter the Hermit & Jack the Giant Killer.

Frederick the Great & Dandy Jim of Caroline.

Brigham Young & the Wandering Jew.

Richard the Third & the Owner of the Race-horse Eclipse.

ODDS AND ENDS. 105

The Man with the Iron Mask & Fanny Ellsler.
Blue Beard & Madame Celeste.
Parson Weems & the Author of The Devil on Two Sticks.
Jack Falstaff & Socrates.
Monsieur Tonson & Thaddeus of Warsaw.
Petroleum Nasby & Confucius.
Daniel Lambert & Tom Thumb
William the Silent & the Youth Chatterton.
Cæsar the Great & Lord Timothy Dexter, with his "Pickle for the Knowing Ones."
Peeping Tom of Coventry & the Man with the Claret-colored Coat.
Ossian, son of Fingal, & Jim Crow.
Joice Heth & Author of Les Miserables.
Cotton Mather & the Witches in Macbeth.
Peter the Great & the Man who struck Billy Patterson.
Beau Brummel & Santa Anna.
Shade of Jo Smith & Deacon Pogram.
Don Quixote & Mother Goose.
Author of the Sorrows of Werter & Peregrini Pickle.
Davy Crockett & Robinson Crusoe.

And numerous others; among whom were the Man in the Moon and his wife, and some people from the Land of Nod.

Commanding this Company of Odd Friends, was the ever-efflorescent, juvenescent Jeems Bukanning, of Old Rye Land. His costume was that of the Continentals of the American Revolution, with shad-bellied blue coat and buckskin breeches. Instead of a cocked hat, however, he wore a conical cap of red leather, twenty inches in height, and surmounted by a yellow, waving plume. In place of a sword, he bore a huge, long-handled tomahawk. He had on a pair of green goggles, fastened back of his head by a chain and padlock. Peter the Hermit was custodian of the key.

Jeems strutted at the head of his company, lifting up each knee alternately to the level of his thigh as he marched, and bringing down each foot regularly with strongly pronounced emphasis to the tap of a drum, while his lofty plume waved like a shaking mandarin.

Immediately behind Jeems, between him and what might be termed his *drag*-oons, was a platoon of *She-caw-geese*. They were also attired in the old Continental style, excepting their caps were green, *balloon*-shaped, and crowned by a tuft of *crow's* feathers. Instead of knapsacks, each had strapped and hanging on his back three or four immense *bladders*, filled with water. This platoon were known as the BLADDERNIERS. They marched in a line with linked arms, and with the same style of leg movement as their commander; but, instead of strutting back as he did, they leaned forward, with their heads down—a necessity of their burdens. Thus it will be seen that the corps, as a whole, when on the march, was a fair specimen of the picturesque grotesque.

Occasionally Jeems halted his company and formed them in a hollow square, facing inward, with himself, grindstone, and Bladderniers in the center, when he turned to and sharpened his tomahawk, for it being the only weapon of war in the corps, he felt keenly the importance of always having it ready in good fighting condition.

On these occasions the Bladderniers stood in line and squirted on the water, while Peeping Tom of Coventry, Ossian, Son of Fingal, the Man who struck Billy Patterson, and Frederick the Great spelled each other in turning the crank.

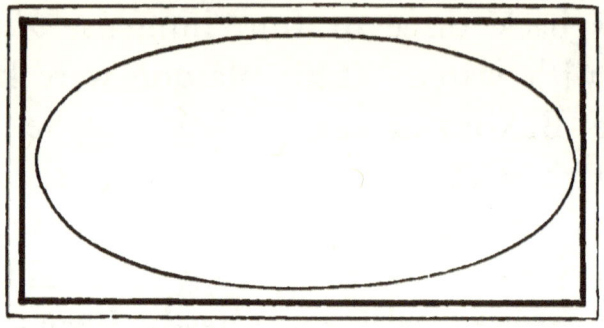

IMAGINARY PICTURE.

Jeems Bukanning, of Old Rye Land, sharpening his tomahawk. He is singing the "Song of the Grindstone," in which he is joined in a chorus by his entire corps of Odd Friends.

When Jeems was sharpening his instrument he always was happy. He generally sang the SONG OF THE GRINDSTONE, in which he was joined in a chorus by his entire corps, the witches in Macbeth and Joice Heath taking the high soprano, while Madame Celeste, Fanny Ellsler, Confucius, and Monsieur Tonson danced a quadrille.

A third company, which succeeded, was entirely composed of "Nobodies," so they mostly assumed the garbs of transcendentals, being attired as gods and goddesses. All the prominent characters in Heathen Mythology were personified, with an intermixture of Satyrs, Fawns, etc.

The rear of this corps consisted of very small people, probably children. They were disguised as fishes, which apparently walked on their tails! They also had their designating knapsacks.

3D COMP'Y.
YE
GODS
AND
LITTLE FISHES.

Uncle Sam's Men followed close after. This corps was composed of the American Congress, and the officers, sailors, soldiers, and marines of the Expedition to Alaska. At their head was Chief Justice S. P. Runafter, who bore a sort of sign-board on a pole,

4TH COMP'Y.
UNCLE SAM'S
MEN.

with the words, "Andy Jinsin—Impeachment!"

> ANDY JINSIN
>
> IMPEACHMENT!

Beside these were many hundred others, including largely of females from Washington and Baltimore. It was estimated one thousand persons were on the ground.

Charles Dickens brought up the rear with his squad, who also bore their designating knapsacks. He had his screen along, and expected to read. It was pictured in tapestry, with the American eagle on its nest. The bird had not hatched much as yet, but was hard at it; looked wise, and promised *big* things.

> YE
>
> DICKENS
>
> SQUAD.

His squad was composed of his agent

ODDS AND ENDS. 111

Dawlbee, David Copperfield, Oliver Twist, Captain Cuttle, and Bunsby, who had ready "an opinion that was an opinion;" also one Nicholas Nickleby, who had been supercargo for Captain Cook in his voyage around the world, and a few others.

IMAGINARY PICTURE.

Max Marattlezak operating upon his new musical instrument, the "Mewonica."

These various corps had standards lettered like their knapsacks, with artistic devices, and in brilliant colors.

The procession halted and formed a ring

around Max Marattlezak, who explained the new musical instrument he had with him, the "Mewonica." Sixteen cats—eight Thomas and eight Sally cats—were selected with reference to their vocal qualities when combined in a choir, and placed in a long box with partitions for each, with holes in front for their heads to project, and others in the rear through which hung their "handles," as they were technically termed.

The instrument was operated upon by squeezing their handles in milk-maid fashion. To tune it up for a performance was a nice operation, and for which purpose a young Pole of great power of grip and a musical ear of unusual delicacy was employed.

By an ingenious contrivance, neither the heads nor the "handles" of the musicians could be withdrawn at option, nor could any of the sixteen be excused on a plea of colds from a concert until after the reserved seats had been taken and a full house secured.

To appreciate this music, required an ear cultivated to a higher degree than ordinary. When a community had once been educated *up* to the standard, no melody was like it. In consequence of so many unappreciating persons leaving in the midst of the concerts, Max had to abate the disturbing nuisance by the issue, at double price, of "*exit* tickets."

The Mewonica had a decided advantage over the opera. The latter illustrates by its music but one *tale;* the Mewonica the burden of many.

Max squoze out for them a few of his choice tunes. They were delighted. Andy Jinsin suggested it as a remedial agent for the Government Hospitals; it would have a soothing effect upon the "Constitution."

Jawge H. Pendletum and Valhanghim at once engaged the Mewonica for the fall campaign of the Unterrified and Screeching.

And Carl Rosa played upon the violin, while Madame Parepa sang:

> "Oh! potatoes they are small,
>   Over there! over there!
> 'Cause they plants 'em in the fall,
>   Over there! over there!
> And eats 'em, tops and all,
>   Over there! over there!"

CHAPTER G.

Which shows the people had "a good time;" describes the race around the Base Ball circle between Andy Jinsin and Jeems Bukanning of Old Rye Land, with the catastrophe to Andy, and his deliverance by a Greek philosopher; the Grand Dinner, at which Andy runs the bee-line of the table, 400 feet long, to embrace General Grent, at the other end, when he falls dead, and is brought to life after revolving many circles, by the Awful Unknown, with his mysterious serpent wand.

IT was a gala day, and so the folks went in for a good time. Pitching quoits, shooting turkies as a mark, crossing a field blindfold, "innocent" games of cards under the trees, martelle, croquet, ten-pins, and base ball were in active operation. Knots of mere talkers were seen here and there: some men talked dollars; some women dress—none scandal! Bursts of laughter now and then arose as some wag got off a funny thing. It was observed the most boisterous groups consisted of only men. These were generally gathered around some venerable old gentlemen with a Saturnine visage. And if, perchance, any inquisitive female, allured by their merriment, approached within ear-shot of such, a Sabbath-like silence at once ensued—a phenomena that was *inexplicable*.

The members of the Companies of Odd Friends, Ye Gods and Little Fishes, scattered here and there in the crowd, gave a rather eccentric appearance to things. The day was quite warm, so the Bladderniers made themselves useful with their novel, well-filled canteens, and won golden opinions for their amiable, obliging dispositions.

At the termination of an exciting game of base ball, a foot race ensued around the course, which attracted every body from the esteem in which the participants were held. These were Jeems Bukanning and Andy Jinsin. Jeems took the lead, when Andy, who had stiffly crooked his elbow, illustrated how wine works wonders, for he passed him at the second base, and had nearly arrived at the home base, when trouble ensued, and what *never* occurred before, a *woman* was at the bottom of it. Secretary Stunem was at the outer edge, near the end of the line, when happening to turn for

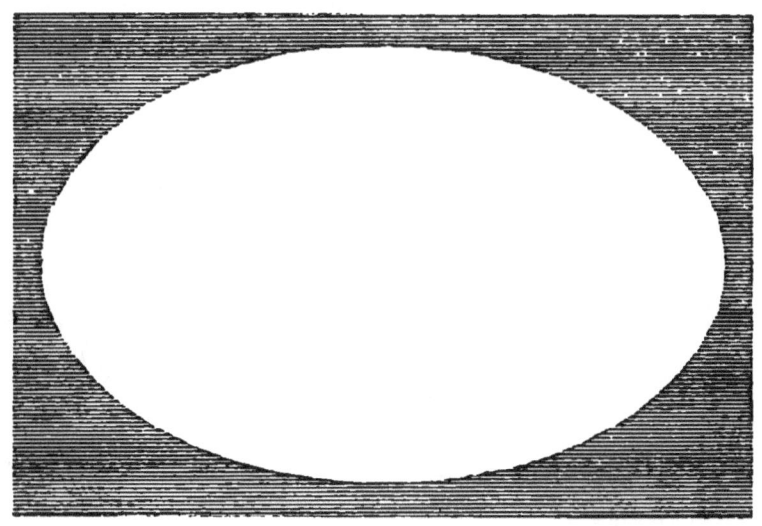

IMAGINARY PICTURE.

Jeems Bukanning and Andy Jinsin run a foot race on the base ball circle.

some purpose, he espied a lady acquaintance in the crowd, whom he had not before seen. With gentlemanly instinct, he tipped his hat, and undulated into the curve of courtesy and recognition. His person was thus partially catapulted within the circle, just as Andy came up. So unexpected was it, that Andy ran full tilt against the Honorable Mr. Stunem, received a dreadful blow in the stomach, which instantly doubled him up, and he fell with a heavy *ugh!*

And Carl Rosa played upon the violin, while Madame Parepa sang:

> "There was an old chap
>   In the West Countre'e,
> A flaw in his lease,
>   The lawyers had found."

As Andy fell, Jeems came up blowing and puffing, his face scarlet as a beet, passed the prostrate man, and with two terrific leaps, considering his gout, completed the circle amid cheers.

And Carl Rosa played upon the violin, while Madame Parepa sang:

> "It was all about felling
>   Of 5 oak trees,
>   And building a house
>   Upon his own ground."

When Andy, gathering himself up, with his hands upon his bowels, moved slowly off, gnashing his teeth, and howling with pain and rage. He had scarcely got sixty yards, when,

ODDS AND ENDS. 119

without any perceptible cause, he again fell, and with another heavy *ugh!* As he dropped, a sudden darkness came over the landscape, black as when night and the storm fiends are abroad. The multitude were appalled, and not a sound was heard, except an occasional groan from Andy.

IMAGINARY PICTURE.

Diogenes in search of an honest man, by the aid of his lantern, finds him in the prostrate Andy.

Finally, a solitary and distant light appeared, as if in the heavens. It moved slowly in a winding form, as if borne by some being. It was, and he was simply descending a mountain, and approaching them. Nearer and nearer came the light, until they descried a tall, venerable personage, with a lofty, intellectual expression, and clothed in white, in the garb of an ancient Greek philosopher. He passed through the crowd with the air of one in search for something. On reaching the prostrate Andy, he cast the light of his lantern full upon the face of him we *love* so well; upon which he started back and raised his arms in joy! Then holding out his light at arms length, he slowly revolved on his heels, until he had described seven distinct circles. As he completed each, he called out in deep, sepulchral tones, ΕΤΡΗΚΑ! which was all GREEK to the multitude. On completing the seventh circle his light instantly expired.

And *Carl Rosa played upon the violin, while Madame Parepa sang:*

<blockquote>
DIOGENES his Lantern
Needs no more,
An HONEST MAN is found,
The *search is o'er.*
</blockquote>

In a twinkling, after the light of Diogenes'

lantern expired, the darkness began to dissipate. A rooster, on top of a neighboring well-sweep, gave a lusty "cock-a-doo-dle-doo;" it was echoed by another a quarter of a mile away; and then at varying distances by numerous others, when came full daylight and happiness: but vanished was the philosopher and his lantern, and no one knew when, how, or where! Not so Andy. He was descried in full vigor and usefulness in a grove near by, walking arm in arm with the estimable Mrs. Chubb.

And Carl Rosa played upon the violin, while Madame Parepa sang:

> "Love is a fire
>   That burns and sparkles,
>   As nat'rally in men
>   As in charcoals."

We said the word Diogenes shouted was all Greek to the multitude. To this we must except the renowned SOCRATES. To him it was *nothing!* The poor old gentleman was greatly fatigued with the excitement of the day: so when the darkness came on, his chin suddenly dropped, and he was off to the land of the *Nod*-dies, where he dreamed he was walking in a grove of *hemlocks*, listening to the soughing of the wind through the branches, and meditating upon the vanities of this transitory existence. On awaking, he learned of the unexpected visit of his old townsman, and it required all his philosophy to choke down his chagrin at losing the chance of meeting with him. He thought he should try and keep awake the next time. He said he was particularly anxious to ascertain the name of the *cooper* who made that *tub* Diogenes lived in: he understood it was a remarkably fine piece of workmanship!

Succeeding this were a series of dances, cotillons, contra-dances, Scotch reels, Irish jigs, and the German, winding up with a grand dinner on the green sward, Theodore Tellem going among the people ringing a *bell* and *crying*, "COME TO YOUR FEEDING! COME TO YOUR FEEDING!"

And Carl Rosa played upon the violin, while Madame Parepa sang:

> "Toll! Roland toll
> In old St. Bavon's tower,"

Which so evidently annoyed Theodore, as if he regarded singing his poetry a personal affront, that the words were changed, but not the tune.

And Carl Rosa played upon the violin, while Madame Parepa sang:

> "Little Jack Horner
> Sat in the corner,
>   Eating Christmas pie;"
> When puss bounced in,
> And took him down,
>   And he began to CRY!

On hearing which, Theodore only jingled the louder and *cried* the more. Then they considerately changed both words and tune.

And Carl Rosa played upon the violin, while Madame Parepa sang:

> "John, John, the Piper's son,
> Stole a pig and away he run;
> John was beat and the pig was eat,
> And John ran BAWLING down the street."

This was too hard on Theodore. At once, as if stung on the hand by a bumble-bee, he gave his bell a chuck so high in air that it was said never to have come down again, but to have gone ringing among the stars! The *little* fellow then ran and hid behind a *leafless* mullen stalk until the laugh was over. While there, he wrote a sonorous leader for the *Independent;* subject, *Joys of Andy!*

A single table, four hundred feet long, was spread with good things prepared by cooks sent from a *reputable* source. At this all sat, when the feast of reason and the flow of wine prevailed, and every thing went as merry as Independence Day, amid the musketry of corks, the letting off of speeches, with toasts, songs, and clouds of cigar smoke.

And Carl Rosa played upon the violin, while Madame Parepa sang:

> "Fill the bumper fair,
>   Every drop we sprinkle
>   O'er the brow of Care,
>   Smooths away a wrinkle."

Andy Jinsin and General Grent occupied respectively the two heads of the table. Near the close, Ulysses mounted his end, and with the aside, "We'll fight it out on this line," lifted his glass for a toast. The table rose as one, and held aloft theirs also, when the General exclaimed, in commanding tones:

"*Here's to the Great Accidentosity!*"

And the multitude repeated, as the voice of many waters mingled with much wine:

"THE GREAT ACCIDENTOSITY!"

So the toast was drank, and with a flourish of music from the Mewonica and the brass band from Alaska, joined to a three times three, four times repeated, ending with a brace of terrific tigers and a single wild-cat.

And Carl Rosa played upon the violin, while Madame Parepa sang:

> " Crambambulee—it is the title
>   Of that good drink we love the best,
>   It is the means that prove most vital
>   When evil fortunes us molest;
>   At evening light and morning free,
>   I take my glass Cram-bam-bu-lee—
>   *Cram Bam Bam Bam Bulee.*"

"Encore!" "Encore!" burst on all sides, and in the center, and from the top and bottom. The cock on the well-sweep echoed in another cock-a-doo-dle-doo! in which he was joined by all his neighbors, at their respective varying distances.

And Carl Rosa played upon the violin, while Madame Parepa sang:

> "Lives of GREAT MEN all remind us,
> We can make our lives SUBLIME,
> And, departing, leave behind us
> Footprints in the sands of time."

Andy was overcome by this enthusiastic ovation. He not only had sprinkled, but *washed* the brow of Care in a deluge of bumpers. His heart warmed in ecstasy to-

IMAGINARY PICTURE.

Andy runs the bee-line of the table to embrace Ulysses at the other end, four hundred feet away, knocking over the dishes, and amid cheers, cries, and cat-calls.

ward General Grent for this unexpected honor. He prepared to rush and hug Ulysses to his bosom. Springing on to the table, he spread out his arms ready for the fraternal embrace, and started at the top of his speed for the other end, four hundred feet distant, knocking over, plowing through, scattering and spilling in his race, to the right and to the left, before and behind, boned turkeys, cold ham, sandwiches, jellies, cakes, oyster soups, gravies, pickles, champagne bottles, liquids, tumblers, and dishes of all sorts. And as he ran, the multitude, wild with excitement, cheered him on:

"Go it, Andy!"
"No circle this time!"
"It's a bee-line, Andy!"
"Constitution's coming up, Andy!"

All this amid cries, and groans, and catcalls, with flourishes of music from the brass band and the Mewonica.

On reaching General Grent, Andy clasped him in his arms in frantic enthusiasm; in a second he had recoiled, shocked as if he had embraced a galvanic battery. For a moment he stood upright; his arms raised aloft; head thrown back; eyes, rolled above, hidden under the upper lids; a deathly pallor overspread his countenance, when a few convulsive tremors succeeded, and then he fell backward at full length, crashing upon the table, his body resting upon the debris of the feast, the head itself in a demolished pyramid of ice-cream.

And Carl Rosa played upon the violin, while Madame Parepa sang:

> "He jumped into a bramble-bush,
>   And scratched out both his eyes;
>   And when he saw his eyes were out,"
>   With all his *fuss* and *strain*,
>   Could *never* GRAB another bush,
>   To scratch 'em in again.

The people were at once sobered by this result, so unexpected and so calamitous. Andy's usefulness was at an end. He was dead, dead, dead as a *duck!*

And Carl Rosa played upon the violin, while Madame Parepa sang:

> "Stand by your glasses, men, steady!
>   Here's to the health of the dead already,
>   And *hurra* for the next that dies!"

But no one felt like drinking any more. No one felt like giving a hurra. Death had been among them and taken their shining mark.

And Carl Rosa played upon the violin, while Madame Parepa sang:

"Old Grimes is dead, that good old man,
 We ne'er shall see him more;
 He used to wear an old blue coat
 All buttoned down before."

As these strains died away, one universal wail ascended in unison with dirge-like strains from the brass band, blowing wind instruments, and caterwaulings from the Mewonica.

Some of the wail must have penetrated below, for at once the air was filled with a suffocating sulphureous odor, so that every person, excepting General Grent and Secretary Sewap, numbering one thousand, gentlemen and ladies, simultaneously, as if by military drill, raised their hands to their noses, seized and squoze that member, holding it, as it were, in a vise during the ensuing scenes. Ulysses, by blowing on a *tin whistle*, summoned the corporal of the guard, so the corporal had double duty to perform—to hold his *own nose* and *that* of the General. The venerable Secretary, Mr. Sewap, improvised a tight-squeezing nose-holder in the claw of a *boiled lobster*.

And Carl Rosa played upon the violin, while Madame Parepa sang:

"Nose! nose! what gave thee
That jolly red nose?
Brandy, champagne, and peppermint
Gave me this jolly red nose."

The moment the word "nose" died away in the refrain, cold chills ran through the assemblage at the sudden apparition of a mysterious, unearthly-looking personage, of gigantic stature, by the side of the deceased.

He was enveloped in a long black gown, like that of a friar, with its cowl thrown over his head, with two lofty horn-like projections. His face was of a coppery hue, hard as that of a mask. His nose was hawked, immense, and thin; eye-brows black, heavy, and arching toward the angles of the forehead; his teeth, like fangs, were fully disclosed by a sardonic grin from a mouth that seemed as a yawning sepulcher; jet-black eyes, with pupils gleaming as round shots of fire, finishes this pretty portrait.

Take him all in all, he was a person that would have attracted attention on Broadway

IMAGINARY PICTURE.

The new manual movement to the nose. General Grent, by blowing on a tin whistle, summoned the corporal of the guard, who thus had double duty to perform—to hold his own nose and that of the General, while Secretary Sewap improvised a tight-squeezing nose-holder in the claw of a boiled lobster.

on any sunny afternoon, and had *ample room*, for a promenade. If such an event should happen, they would feel themselves *slighted* down there if he did not finally bring up at the *Herald* office!

His movements were noiseless as a shadow, when, from beneath his cloak, he drew a long wand, around which was writhing a large, powerful snake, its head oscillating to and fro at its farther end, when he began the resuscitation of Andy. As the Unknown mounted the table, General Grent, without any *visible* reluctance, moved out of his way.

Standing up over the dead, he placed the end of his wand to each ear, when the serpent inserted his forked tongue into those orifices and hissed, which Jerry Darkname said seemed to have a reviving influence. The noise was as the escape of vapor from the steam-valve. Then he placed the wand at the crown of Andy's head, and moved it around in a circle, his body following it, and revolving on its center as the needle of the compass revolves on its pivot to a magnet held by a moving hand.

Thus his body swung around, effectually cleaning the table within the circumference.

ODDS AND ENDS. 133

Gradually the Unknown increased the speed, until it whirled so rapidly, circle after circle, that his person seemed but the buzzing wheel of some machine in rapid motion. The gyration having reached its acme, it as gradually

IMAGINARY PICTURE.

The Awful Unknown standing over the dead Andy; brings him to life by his mysterious incantations with his serpent wand.

declined, and finally ceased. Then, with a sudden raising of the wand aloft, *up* came Andy. Not so the snake; for at the same instant he *dropped off* dead. The life that had been in him had gone into Andy. The life still existed, but *not* in a snake's body.

And Carl Rosa played upon the violin, while Madame Parepa sang:

> Hit him hard,
>   For he has no friends
> In the place above,
>   Nor in that beneath;
> Smite him on the right,
>   And smite him on the left.
> Then drop in a settler,
>   By way of cap-sheaf.

When Andy thus arose to his feet, he was restored to his normal condition. His back, however, appeared shocking, from the puddle of liquors and victuals in which he had lain and revolved.

Andy rubbed his eyes, and then looked full upon his unexpected restorer, when his face at once relapsed into an expression of recognition. It was evidently an *old acquaintance*. Mysterious signs passed between them, ending by the Unknown pointing downward with his wand, as if he expected him finally to go below and partake of his *permanent hospitality.* At

ODDS AND ENDS. 135

this Andy shrugged, sniveled, and looked sheepish, while the horrible grin upon the other only widened, as with an exultant air he made a low bow, turned and stalked in silence away, quickly disappearing in a ravine.

As he moved off, something beneath his long, trailing gown behind wagged to and fro, what no one seemed *anxious* to follow and lift up that garment to ascertain.

And Carl Rosa played upon the violin, while Madame Parepa sang:

> "At break of day,
>   A-walking the Devil has gone,
> To visit his snug farm the Earth,
>   And see how his stock goes on.
>
> "And o'er the hill,
>   And o'er the dale,
> The Devil walked,
>   And switched his long tail,
> As a gentleman switches his cane."

Now he was gone, the air became pure, and all could breathe free again. The multitude dropped arms, ceasing the new manual movement to the nose. General Grent dismissed the corporal of the guard, while Mr. Sewap removed his lobster ornament. His nasal organ, for a month after, had a *pinched* expression, finally removed only by frequent and powerful drafts upon his snuff-box.

We omitted to mention that the Unknown picked up the snake and carried it off in his bosom. Jerry Darkname thought it showed signs of life. Perhaps it did. The animal had clearly been dead, but it is probable that the original life which had been Andy's was then going into the serpent. If so, then, when it had all fully got there, its character would change into that harmless kind, called by little children "a GOOD snake."

CHAPTER H.

In which Mr. Dickens reclines under a lofty sugar-maple, where he is visited by birds, and sings an impromptu song, "The Lassie Music;" is joined by little Oliver Twist, with two puppies, and plays with them; finally is captured by Mrs. Grundy, and they talk together, in which he philosophizes and makes odd suppositions, and thereat she calls him "a funny man."

THE people, wearied with these exciting scenes, wanted a change; so that when the proposition was broached that Mr. Dickens should give them a reading, it was received with acclamations. On looking around, that gentleman was nowhere to be seen.

Early in the festival, he had pocketed a few choice Havanas, and strolled into the forest for a quiet ramble. Coming to a lofty sugar-maple, it seemed so inviting there that he folded up his screen for a pillow, and dropping it a yard or so from its shaggy column, laid down on his back on the velvety sward. Casting his eyes upward, he drew in nectar from the noble tree umbrellaed over him; from the fantastic forms of its leaves, the delicacy of their surfaces, their infinite variety of color, the play of light and shade among them as they gently moved in the soft current, the beautiful offspring of rough, grotesque branches, by whom they were strongly and lovingly upheld and sustained during their short, innocent young lives.

IMAGINARY PICTURE.

Mr. Dickens having a good time under the sugar-maple.

He appeared to think there was no view of a tree so soul-entrancing as that one gets when he is on his back, and sees its projecting wings, so soft and tender, spread between him and the skies. He regarded it as one of the infinite texts from which the Great Master continually talks to us, as a solace from our work-day cares.

As he lay there, some little brown chip-

ODDS AND ENDS. 139

birds flew down, and hopped close by him, and picked up crumbs from crackers he had been munching; while, high up among the branches, a plump-breasted robin stretched its little throat and gave him a tune to the music of the woods. Upon this—Carl Rosa and Madame Parepa not being present—the reclining man hummed a couple of impromptu

IMAGINARY PICTURE.

The little brown chip-birds repeating to the author the song "The Lassie Music."

verses, which he never had printed, and so we repeat them as they were given to us the next morning by the two little tame chip-birds, who were so near as to hear them. What the one forgot the other remembered, and what the other forgot the one remembered, so we saved it all. It would have done your heart good to see how proud and happy the wee things were when they opened their tiny mouths and piped it all out to us just as he sang it.

THE LASSIE MUSIC.

'Twas at creation's earliest dawn,
When Music, baby-girl, was born,
The angels danced, the new earth sang,
And all the stars to frolic sprang,
While mamma cried, and papa run
And groaned, because 'twas not a son.

But when to years the lassie grew,
The happiest child the whole world knew,
Her sweet notes trilled so joyously,
And soothed all cares so lovingly,
That mamma laughed, and papa run
And danced, because 'twas not a son.

Just then, up came young Oliver Twist with two dogs of only a few weeks terrestrial existence. As he lay flat upon the sward, the puppies pounced upon Mr. Dickens in great glee, ran over him, pulled his beard and hair with their bits of teeth, and performed the many joyous antics so comical and pleasing to see in these confiding, merry little creatures.

In this situation, he was surprised by a party in search, captured, and taken back to give them a reading. Among his captors was a lady, the rich widow of one Jenkins Grundy, who lived in a marble palace on Fifth Avenue. She was a personage who always had "her say" about every thing, so she had it on this occasion, which led to a conversation between them. It is all here reported:

"Oh, my! its *funny* to see a gentleman like you playing with dogs."

"Madame," replied Mr. Dickens, "we read in the good book that man was made but a little lower than the angels, and that all animals were placed under his dominion. Man, therefore, is thus midway between the angels and them; so, whenever they require protection, we are their angels. This mysterious thing we call life is made up of little things. Nothing that the Eternal Mind occupies itself in creating is too minute for our study. You saw me amusing myself with those little animals. Their comical antics, their innocence, their confidence gave me exquisite pleasure. When a noble dog comes up, joyously wagging his tail, and places his paw in my hand, as much as to say, 'How do you do, Mr. Dickens?' and then looks up wistfully in my face, as though reading my thoughts, and as though, too, he loved me, and wanted me to feel he loved me, my heart goes out toward him. I have such an intense desire to learn the thoughts and emotions that occupy his mind, that, for the sake of this knowledge, to enable me more fully to sympathize with him, I would gladly for one hour be a dog!"

"Oh, my! Mr. Dickens, what a *funny man* you are!"

"Perhaps so, Madame. If I then remained a dog all the rest of my days, maybe I should be more worthy of affection than many who walk the earth in pride and power."

"If that ever occurs, I shall want *you* to come and live at my country-seat, on the North River, and be *my* watch-dog."

"I agree to that, on the condition that you take good care of me, and not drive me away when I go and jump up and put my paw out for a hearty squeeze, and wag my tail, and then look up so lovingly in your face, as though it was the sweetest, most darling face in all the wide, wide world!"

"Oh, law me! why, what a man you are! I could n't have the heart to push you away."

"Another thing, you must feed me well. No old, dry bare bones and spoiled meat will do for me! I have got a delicate stomach, Madame, a delicate stomach, and always have had."

"What will you want?"

"Madame, you must recollect I am an Englishman."

And Carl Rosa played upon the violin, while Madame Parepa sang:

"Fee, faw, fie, fum,
    I smell the blood of an Englishman,
    And be he dead or be he alive,
    I must have some."

"What of that?" inquired Mrs. Grundy.

"Being an Englishman, I must have my *mutton-chops* every morning for breakfast;

otherwise, I shall go to your sheep pasture and help myself."

"You shall have your mutton-chops for breakfast."

IMAGINARY PICTURE.

Portrait of Mr. Dickens as he would appear if he was changed into a dog.

"Oh! I must have, beside, 'English breakfast tea,' a couple of boiled 'heggs,' some stale bread, a boiled potato, and a morning daily."

"You shall be accommodated, sir. I take the *Herald*, and you can have that to read."

"I trust it is a good paper. If it is one of those vile sheets your people sometimes publish, it would destroy my appetite for my mutton-chops and 'heggs.' Beside, Madame, I shall have a *reputation* to support. Although I shall be 'only a dog,' yet I shall expect to be a respectable dog, and could n't be seen reading a sheet that did not uphold the right and *stamp upon the wrong.*"

"I appreciate your delicacy," replied Mrs. Grundy.

"And then I must have *roast beef* every day for dinner," continued Mr. Dickens.

"You shall have it, sir."

"Beside, I must have a bottle of XX London Stout to wash it down."

"Agreed, Mr. Dickens; and I will also lay in a good supply of Worcestershire sauce, old Stilton cheese, and as much ''alf and 'alf,' all the time, as you can drink; and then, if you get sick, I shall send for my family doctor."

"Madame, it will be unnecessary for you ever to send for your family doctor. I'm never sick, excepting I sometimes am liable to fainting turns, when the *smell* of roast beef invariably brings me to. All you will have to do, if such a thing should happen, is to roast a bit of beef, and bring it, *hot* and *sissing*, and put under my nose; then I shall recover with the first scent. It always goes right to *the spot*."

"It shall be done; and then you'll be my faithful, loving New Foundland, wont you?"

"No Madame," answered Mr. Dickens, "I sha'n't. I tell you I'm an Englishman." And then in deep, gruff tones he added: "Can't be any thing but a BULL!"

"Oh!" exclaimed Mrs. Grundy, "an awful, great, savage bull-dog! I should be scared to death at the sight of you!"

"No you wouldn't, Madame. I admit my growl would be *terrible!* but I wouldn't hurt any body. If I found small boys up in your cherry-trees stealing your ox-hearts, I should at once catch them by the waist-band, and nowhere else. Then I should pass up to them a *note* from you, neatly written on gilt-edged paper, with a great G printed upon it in a rustic letter, presenting your compliments, and requesting the young gentlemen to continue eating your cherries until they were satisfied. It is probable they would then eat voraciously, until they all got the *stomach-ache dreadfully,* for which I should be sorry; but they would never again tear their breeches by

ODDS AND ENDS. 147

climbing into your cherry-trees without permission."

"A capital idea that, Mr. Dickens. What a *funny man* you are!"

"That's what I call the TREATMENT OF CRIME ON THE KINDNESS SYSTEM."

"Oh! what a *funny man!*"

"Yes, I suppose I am funny; but let us philosophize a little. The Good Being has arranged affairs here so that things which require our services *win* us by their qualities. There is no quality that so draws us toward any living object as its *weakness*. While I was down under that tree, some little chip-birds lit by me, and one, with a surprising tameness, hopped so near that I could have grasped it in my hands and crushed it; but in its very *weakness was its strength*. Its strength was in the moral power it exerted

IMAGINARY PICTURE.

Portrait of the dog Dickens in the act of arresting the young cherry thieves.

over me to protect the weak, the feeble, and the ignorant. You see the idea, do you?"

"Yes, sir; but what a *funny man!* I never!"

"Now," continued Mr. Dickens, "just transform that chip-bird into a bird of the size of yonder Ark, with strength corresponding, but the same bird as before in spirit and qualities. It is no longer weak, but strong. Your feelings at once change. It becomes a hideous monster."

"Oh! awful! I should run and scream! I am afraid it would take me for a worm, seize me, and eat me up!"

"Not at all, Madame. Though the good book says we are all worms, yet I do n't think the monster would make that mistake in your case. He would take you for something prettier than that—for something *very* beautiful."

And as he said this, Mr. Dickens looked at the flounces, furbelows, trail, jewelry, and brilliant, gorgeous attire of the lady. It took five thousand dollars in value in dry goods to cover the nakedness of her person

ODDS AND ENDS. 149

from the world, but it would exhaust more than all the bank-vaults in Christendom to conceal the nakedness of her mind.

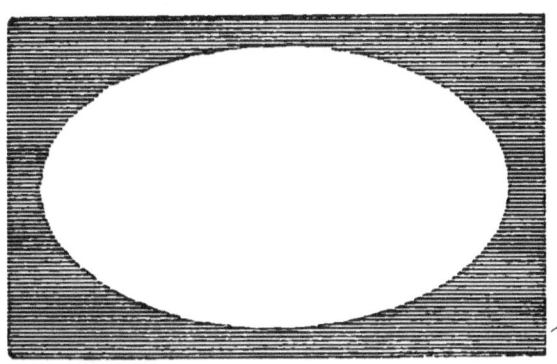

IMAGINARY PICTURE.

How Mrs. Grundy looked when Mr. Dickens told her what the chip-bird would take her for if the chip-bird became of the size of the Ark.

"What would he take me for?" she inquired.

"A BUTTERFLY!"

When he said this, he dropped his chin on his breast, rolled up his eyes at Mrs. Grundy, and puckered his mouth into an O. That enchanting creature at the same moment threw up her hands, laid back her head, and drawled out at the top of her register, "OH, MY!" ending with a little, empty giggle.

And Carl Rosa played upon the violin, while Madame Parepa sang:

"I'd be a butterfly, born in a bower,
  Where roses, and lilies, and jessamine meet,
 Roving about from flower to flower,
  And sipping each bud that seems most sweet."

CHAPTER I.

In which Mr. Dickens continues his conversation with Mrs. Grundy, and philosophizes farther upon the power of weak things; describes the wonderful success of the laughing doctor, and ends with stating what Mrs. Grundy one day put in her pipe and smoked.

MR. DICKENS continued his benevolent talk with Mrs. Grundy by saying:
"I admire a noble-spirited race-horse; but my heart goes out to the poor work-horse, that has a hard time, yet, withal, is patient and uncomplaining. I admire a splendid, well-developed gentleman, with great, strong qualities, that give him place and power; but my heart goes out to the laboring man that I see go by in the morning, with his dinner-kettle on his arm, to work, maybe, all day in a dingy shop, amid dirt, smoke, and dust, the continuous whang of trip-hammers, and the horrid clang of tools on iron from morn till night, and this year after year his life through.

"Poor fellow! it is but little he gets out of this beautiful world! But when a cultivated man, who is never known to make the first sacrifice for the weak, with honeyed words uses the ignorance of such to elevate himself to place and power, and then advocates principles that still further crushes the humble, my heart does not go out to him—not very much; at any rate, if it does, it do n't stay out long; it comes in before it rains.

"Let me further show this principle, for the world is full of illustrations. As you walk in your garden at your country-seat, you admire the flowers as they bloom in tints of glory. After a little you come, maybe, to a pile of stones, and you find between them a rose-bud, and it, as it were, pouts out its little, thin, red lips, and says, in a modest, trembling voice, 'Good lady, I am a tiny, wee thing; pray do move away these great stones, and give me a chance to live and grow. If you but will, I shall be a great, elegant flower one of these days, and have a good time.'

"Your heart goes out to it, and you stoop down and roll away the stones from its sepulcher; and, day after day, you tend it, and think more of it than all the rest of the flowers in the garden, for it is the weak child. You thus become the angel of the rose-bud, and you prepare it for heaven—that is, the heaven of flowers, which is to bloom in loveliness, and fill the air with fragrance."

"I always was fond of flowers," said Mrs. Grundy. "Oh, I do think you are a *funny man!*"

"When an infant enters life it cries. The mother's first feeling is pity for its helplessness. Out of that pity comes the sweetest thing on earth—a mother's love. And in the depths of that feeling, she runs to exaggeration and hyperbole. After exhausting the vocabulary of praise, she turns to that of abuse, and threatens to eat it up, or to bite off its nose, or do some other wicked act."

"I never did any such thing. I always turned over my children to their nurses. But I do think you are a *funny man!*"

"I am a funny man," replied Mr. Dickens, "and so I will talk a little more."

"Oh, do! I love to hear you; you are *so funny!*"

"Nothing touches me as the sight of children as I walk on the streets; especially a group of little girls of humble parentage, chatting together on their way to school, with their arms gathered in front, holding slate and books, and their shawls drawn "scrooching" over their shoulders. I always pause to look at such, to listen to their sweet, young voices, to watch the motions of their delicate, slender feet and ankles from beneath their drapery, and the quick, agile movements of their lithe figures. I think, oh! how beautiful, and then so young! so innocent, so unsuspecting! Some of you will have a hard lot in life; some mated to coarse, brutal men; others, perhaps, to fall by the way-side, and to become that most desolate of all things— a crushed human flower."

And Carl Rosa played upon the violin, while Madame Parepa sang:

"One more unfortunate,
Weary of breath,
Rashly importunate,
Gone to her death!

> Take her up tenderly,
> Lift her with care!
> Fashioned so slenderly—
> Young and so fair!"

"Such reputation as I have," Mr. Dickens continued, "arises from my recording facts in the condition of humble people, which the sympathetic every-where also observe. I reflect much upon what I see, turn things over in my mind until I get them in odd, strange connections, and so often amuse people by presenting them in that way; but, as I see them first, I have the *first* laugh. When I am thinking over scenes for a book, amusing relations of things will strike my mind, and showing it in my expression as I walk the floor, my children will look up in my face pleased, and inquire, 'Papa, what makes you smile so?' and I reply, 'O, it's some little Tomfoolery; you will see it all in a book one of these days.'

"This world," continued Mr. Dickens, "is full of sad, terrible things, and the sensibilities of the good are continually oppressed by the knowledge of wrong, oppression, and suffering every-where. Beside, every heart has its own fountain of sorrow, and those most susceptible to joy are, from the very delicacy of their organizations, most susceptible to anguish. As a relief to human woes, the Good Being has implanted in our natures the faculty of appreciating and being benefited by HUMOR. No medicine so quickly relieves an aching heart as a hearty laugh; and if your people all read my books, and laughed as much in reading as I do in writing them, your doctors would be out of business in six months.

"I once knew an old doctor whose entire stock in trade consisted of bread pills and a collection of FUNNY STORIES. Soon as he had felt of a patient's pulse, and got him to run out his tongue, he would say: 'Pooh! there aint much the matter with you! You are a great deal *more well* than you are sick; if you were not, you would n't be *here*. We'll fix you up in short meter.'

"Then he would open his repository of stories. All the family, and the neighbors, too, learning of his presence by his old chaise out in front, would, by this time have gathered in the room, and filled it to overflowing, to take some of his medicine—they did *love* it so! It kept them in health, warded off all kinds of diseases, as dyspepsia, liver complaints, neuralgia, *barrenness of pocket*, etc. Nobody could *feel* poor when he was about, no matter *how* rich they were.

"He was much troubled, as he walked about the town, by people who stopped him on the corners, and 'button-holed' him, so as to get some of his medicine without paying for it. It was very dishonest, but there is no accounting for the meanness of some folks!

"A single visit from him generally cured the patient. This mode of treatment resulted disastrously for the Doctor; he worked himself entirely *out* of *practice!* People learned it did n't pay to be sick when he was around, so he had to go to another town, and the same thing resulted there, and he was obliged again to move. Poor man! it kept him nothing but a rolling stone all the days of his life!"

"He then should have altered his method of practice," suggested Mrs. Grundy.

"Oh! he wanted to, for his family's sake,

for he had a quantity of growing children, and continually changing their schools made it bad for them, but he couldn't."

"Why not?" inquired Mrs. Grundy.

IMAGINARY PICTURE.

The Laughing Doctor administering his medicine.

"You see," answered Mr. Dickens, "he had unconsciously taken so *much* of his own medicine, that the muscles of his cheeks had all shortened, so that the power of looking *anxious* and *solemn* by the bedside of the sick was completely gone. Nobody could see him without laughing; the expression of his countenance was so irresistibly comical.

"Beside, he was an exceedingly modest man, of exquisitely delicate sensibilities, and had rather die than to go around prying into things, and asking people about their private, internal arrangements, as do other doctors. He knew it was all useless. He was too conscientious to resort to the old way, when he felt he could always cure by his mode of treatment. So, like all reformers, he became a martyr to his own principles."

"That was hard," said Mrs. Grundy.

"Yes, Madame, very. Beside, he made a great many enemies."

"Why, you astonish me! How, on the earth, could that be?"

"Nothing more natural, Madame. The patent medicine manufacturers, all sorts of doctors, as allopathic, hydropathic, homeopathic, botanic, eclectic, clairvoyant, euroscopic, etc.; the apothecaries, undertakers, sextons, and the mourning dry goods people *hated* him with a perfect hatred. You see, he ruined their business and brought distress upon their families."

"I do n't wonder," replied Mrs Grundy.

"There were two classes of patients, however, he never could cure, but these everywhere were too limited in number to furnish his support."

"What were they?"

"Those who *fell* from heights, and had their brains dashed out by striking the ground too *suddenly*, and those who had *fits*."

"Why not?" inquired Mrs. Grundy.

"You see, to have the Doctor's medicine take a good hold, required some intellect. People who fell from heights were deficient— deficient in *understanding*, or else they never would have suffered from that cause."

"O yes, O yes!" chimed in Mrs. G.; "but how about fits?"

"The Doctor could not cure fits by his mode of treatment. He could only *change* their character."

"How so?"

"He changed them into *laughing fits*," replied Mr. Dickens. "And he lost several patients in that way; and it was *meanly* thrown up against him by his enemies, for they DIED A-LAUGHING!"

"Oh! oh!"

Upon saying which, Mrs. Grundy suddenly drew up her face and put her handkerchief up to her eyes, as if about to burst into tears. A puff of wind had just at that instant filled them with dust, and the pain for a few moments was excruciating. She had our sympathy.

IMAGINARY PICTURE.

One of the Laughing Doctor's patients in his death agonies.

At this time they had arrived on the ground, where the multitude were all on the *qui vive* for the new sensation; and they had enough, as you will see further on.

As for Mrs. Grundy, when she got home to her mansion on Fifth Avenue, she one day retired to a corner, put a well-filled pipe in her mouth, seated herself on a low chair, leaned forward, placed her elbows on her knees, her wrists met under her chin, while her outstretched palms covered her cheeks, and thus supported in that attitude, she sat and smoked the whole matter that Mr. Dickens had told her; and the smoke thereof arose, and ever after remained, it is to be hoped, a grateful incense in her presence.

IMAGINARY PICTURE.

How Mrs. Grundy will look if you take her by the chin and ask her "what she says."

If you doubt it, the next time you meet her take her chin between your fore-finger and thumb, give it a few good-natur'd shakes, and ask her; and then you'll hear what the whole world is anxious to know, "WHAT MRS. GRUNDY SAYS!" Then you will please report it, and we'll write another book, and then they will say, "WHAT A FOOL!"

CHAPTER J.

Mr. Dickens prepares to give a reading, during which he takes a pinch of titillating powder, and displays a new pattern of a handkerchief; after which there is opened, stretched wide open, ready for use, quite a considerable quantity of fly-traps.

THERE being no regular stage for reading, a substitute was found for Mr. Dickens in the omnibus stage which had brought Andy and party in the morning. Ralph Waldo Emmerem, Harry Wood Beachem, Oliver Wendell Humes, and William Gilmore Sammies were sent around with their hats for a collection. It was thought these four gentlemen, with double-dose names, would put the financial matter through with eminent success; but Dawlbee, dissatisfied, sent out little Oliver Twist, with a platter which had escaped the plowing operations of Andy, "for more," but we do not think Mr. Dickens ever knew of it.

Andy Jinsin, arm in arm with Mrs. Chubb; Secretary Sewap and Jerry Darkname, each also with a lady, with other gentlemen and ladies from Washington, got into the stage—or rather we should say under the platform—that they might be near to hear. The four gentlemen with double-dose names mounted to the top, together with many others, among whom were David Copperfield, Captain Cuttle, Bunsby, one Nicholas Nickleby (who had been supercargo for Captain Cook in his voyage around the world), Jeems Bukanning, of Old Rye Land, Peeping Tom of Coventry, two "Gods," and one "Little Fish."

All these seated themselves around on the outer margin of the 'bus, with their backs to the center, forming a continuous balustrade for Mr. Dickens' protection, while their overhanging line of legs, ending with a display of boots, made a picturesque fringe to the concern.

Mr. Dickens, feeling the want of a table, three small boys of graded size and age—viz.: eight, ten, and twelve years—volunteered, and felt themselves honored to supply the deficiency. Placing themselves in the posture of all-fours, one above the other, the largest at bottom and the smallest on top, every thing was ready.

IMAGINARY PICTURE.

Mr. Dickens about to give a reading from an omnibus stage. The stage has a protecting balustrade in a line of bodies on its margin, fringed with legs ending with a display of pendant boots. His table is formed of three boys, respectively twelve, ten, and eight years of age, placed on all-fours, the smallest on top.

As Mr. Dickens laid his MSS. on the back of the little eight-year old as a table-top, the oddity of the thing made his eyes twinkle with suppressed merriment. Blushing and biting his lips, however, he was about to begin, when his attention was arrested by the sight of an arm thrust at full length through the "poke-up" hole, back of the driver's seat, holding in its hand a small silver box containing a titillating powder. At the same time he heard from below the voice of the owner of the arm and box, calling to him by name. It was the small, piping voice of Mr. Sewap, drawling out in blandest tones:

"M-i-s-t-e-r D-i-c-k-e-n-s, w-i-l-l y-o-u h-a-v-e a p-i-n-c-h t-o r-e-f-r-e-s-h y-o-u-r-s-e-l-f b-e-f-o-r-e y-o-u b-e-g-i-n y-o-u-r r-e-a-d-i-n-g?"

Whereupon Mr. Dickens went up to that box and took therefrom a pinch of snuff, which act of acceptance had a soothing effect upon Mr. Sewap. He felt in his conscience he had done a good thing. Then and there, standing upon that 'bus, in the presence of the assembled multitude, every eye upon him to see how he did it, Mr. Dickens took that pinch, and it seemed to do him good, and that assembled multitude felt good at his evident refreshment. Then and there drawing a handkerchief from his breast pocket, Mr. Dickens

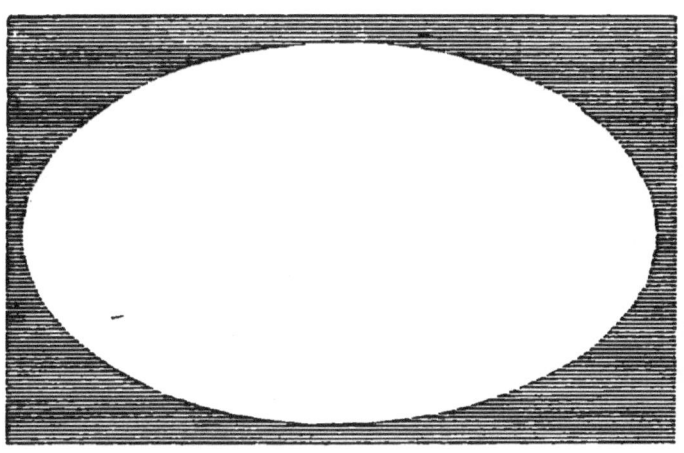

IMAGINARY PICTURE.

Mr. Dickens displaying that handkerchief with a chain border, embroidered with scarlet silk, and the center a crescent moon, embroidered in green silk.

held it up by the corners, so that every lady in that assembled multitude—several hundred in all—observed it was a *white* handkerchief, *with a chain border, embroidered with scarlet silk, and the center a crescent moon, embroidered in green silk!* and they each and all, then and there, resolved to embroider some handkerchiefs, after the same pattern, for their husbands and gentlemen loves. Then and there Mr.

Dickens took that handkerchief loosely in the palm of his hand, and, in the presence of the assembled multitude, every eye upon him to see how he did it, and he knowing it, too, without the least embarrassment, lifted that handkerchief with a *chain border, embroidered in scarlet silk, and the center a crescent moon, embroidered in green silk*, and, without considering the indelicacy of the thing—*wiped!*

And *Carl Rosa played upon the violin, while Madame Parepa sang:*

>"Fire on the mountains!
>Run, boys, run!
>Cat's in the cream-pitcher!
>Come, girls, come!"

Yes, actually wiped, with measured deliberation, for it was a warm day, the perspiration from his forehead!

>"This he did, and nothing more."

Returning that handkerchief with a *chain border, embroidered with scarlet silk, and the center a crescent moon, embroidered in green silk*, to his pocket, Mr. Dickens made a graceful obeisance, threw back his head, and opened his mouth to begin, when that member remained fixed, stretched wide open, as if he *heard something!* The four gentlemen with double-dose names simultaneously threw back their heads and opened their mouths, and they remained fixed, stretched wide open, as if they *heard something!* David Copperfield, Captain Cuttle, Bunsby, and one Nicholas Nickleby (who had been supercargo for Captain Cook in his voyage around the world), Jeems Bukanning, of Old Rye Land, Peeping Tom of Coventry, two "Gods," and one "Little Fish," simultaneously threw back their heads and opened their mouths, and they remained fixed, stretched wide open, as if they *heard something!*

All on the 'bus did the same, excepting the three small boys of graded sizes and respectively twelve, ten, and eight years of age, who could n't throw back their heads, but opened their mouths, and they remained fixed, stretched wide open, as if they *heard something!* Those under the platform, in the 'bus—Andy Jinsin, Mrs. Chubb, Mr. Sewap, Jerry Darkname, (each with a lady,) and the other gentlemen and ladies from Washington—simultaneously threw back their heads and opened their mouths and they remained fixed, stretched wide open, as if they *heard something!*

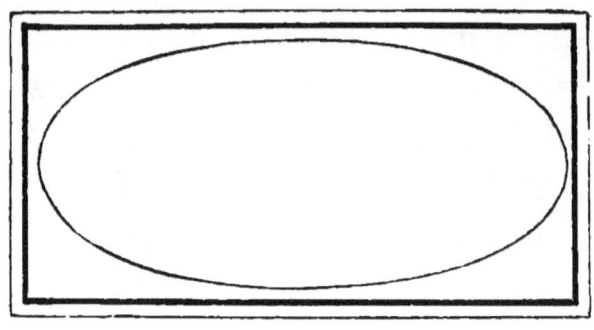

IMAGINARY PICTURE.

Quite a collection of fly-traps opened.

Every person in that vast assemblage, numbering one thousand gentlemen and ladies, as was estimated, simultaneously threw back their heads and opened their mouths, and they remained fixed, stretched wide open, as if they *heard something!*

Including Mr. Dickens, the four gentlemen with double-dose names, David Copperfield, Captain Cuttle, Bunsby, and one Nicholas Nickleby (who had been supercargo for Captain Cook in his voyage around the world), Jeems Bukanning, of Old Rye Land, Peeping Tom of Coventry, two "Gods," and one "Little Fish;" all others on the 'bus—counting in the three small boys of graded sizes, and respectively twelve, ten, and eight years of age—those under the platform, in the 'bus—Andy Jinsin, Mrs. Chubb, Mr. Sewap, Jerry Darkname, (each with a lady,) and the other ladies and gentlemen from Washington—every person in that vast assemblage, numbering one thousand persons, ladies and gentlemen, as was estimated—including all these, we say, there was thus simultaneously opened, and they remained fixed, stretched wide open, ready for instant use, quite a collection of FLY-TRAPS!

And Carl Rosa played upon the violin, while Madame Parepa sang:

> "There's a good time coming,
> There's a good time coming, boys!
> Wait a little longer."

It was but a little longer they had to wait; not a century, nor a decade, nor a year, nor a month, nor a week, nor a day, nor an hour, nor a minute. The good time promised was "over the left," and it arrived in five seconds, when ceased their dreadful suspense.

CHAPTER K.

The Awful Unknown sets loose all the animal population of the Ark, just as Mr. Dickens opens his mouth to read, when they charge wildly down upon the multitude, who flee in terror; and many strange things happen.

SUSPENSE ended is, in a measure, a relief, although the change may come through instant suffering. Any thing, we all say, but the agony of waiting the descent of the uplifted club.

When the dread suspense under which the multitude labored had terminated, every heart was struck with terror, every cheek blanched, and every nerve quivered, for the astounding fact burst upon them that the whole animal population of the Ark had been let loose, were coming ashore, and charging down wildly upon them ! Then was revealed the meaning of that horrible, mysterious, hellish leer upon the face of the Unknown, as he stalked triumphantly away, noiseless as a fallen spirit, and disappeared in the dark, gloomy recesses of the ravine. He meant mischief, and had now gone and did it!

IMAGINARY PICTURE.

The Grand Hegira. The animals broke loose from the Ark, and charging down wildly upon the crowd, who break and run in terror.

In a moment the birds filled the air with their flutterings and screechings—crows, hawks, eagles, condors, buzzards, snipes, cat-birds, and much poultry. On came the others full tilt. The bulls bellowed, the hyenas screamed, the lions roared, the wolves howled, the sheep bleated, the jackasses brayed, the baboons chattered, and every other beast and bird that had a voice joined in the din.

The ground, too, at once became alive with serpents, squirming, hissing, and shooting out their forked tongues; rattlesnakes, vipers, black-snakes, cobra de capellos, hooded snakes, copperheads, and all others of the horrid, squirming generation.

The multitude could not tarry for the luscious new wine that was to have been poured out for their thirsty souls, but, as one, partook of the panic and went. And they didn't stand on the order of their going, but went at once, hastened on in their flight by multitudes of stinging insects, as wasps, hornets, bumble-bees, with the lesser annoyances of clouds of gallinippers, horse-flies, and devils' darning-needles.

Max Marattlezak took "the lead." He whipped his horses in a frenzy and disappeared from the scene, while the performers in the Mewonica sent up discordant cries. To the tail of the wagon hung Jeems Bukanning, and also Andy Jinsin, who had run away from Mrs. Chubb, leaving that estimable lady in the lurch.

After them, running at full speed, were Jefferson Devis, General Grent, the omnibus stage driver, Ben Walkonbottom, Admiral Sammies, Grandmamma Wulles, and the entire multitude, including the "Mutual Friends," "Odd Friends," "Ye Gods and Little Fishes," "Uncle Sam's Men," "Ye Dickens' Squad," the Noah family, Ripstiwizen Van Winkle and his dog Snyder, and Brick Pummice, who lost a new hat.

And Carl Rosa played upon the violin, while Madame Parepa sang:

> "The little dog laughed
> To see the sport,
> And the dish ran away
> With the spoon."

The only vehicle, beside that which held the Mewonica, was an Adams' Express wagon, which brought off in safety Commodore Vanderconstruct, Ledger Bonny, and some people from the Land of Nod. In the van of the runaways was the deputation of She-caw-geese.

The most terror-stricken of the host was, undoubtedly, the Wandering Jew, for his fears were spiritual. He fancied the incensed spirits of his six hundred and thirty-one deceased wives were after him, which they undoubtedly were.

The Man in the Moon and his wife escaped by climbing up to their habitation on a bean-stalk which had fastened itself around on one of the horns of the moon. It grew from a miraculous bean that had dropped through a hole in the pocket of Jack the Giant Killer on his arrival.

IMAGINARY PICTURE.

The Man in the Moon and his wife escaping by climbing up to their habitation on the bean-stalk of Jack the Giant Killer.

At the first alarm, Harry Wood Beachem and Jawge H. Pendletum, who had continued through the entire day their duties as nurses with a tenderness and assiduity which did them honor, unconsciously threw away their young charges into a large clump of barberry bushes. The Pre-Adamite Van Winkle rescued them; and, what is more, when the enemy got too near that venerable individual and his dog Snyder, both paused and turned around, when the dog barked, and Van Winkle brought his gun to bear in a menacing attitude upon their four-footed, two-footed, flying, and wriggling pursuers. They were, however, in no great danger, for the extreme age of the dog had left him with only gums, and that load had been in Mr. Van Winkle's fowling-piece over a million of years!

Wendell Feelups turned also, and tried the effect of a round cussing. He cussed with a vehemence that enhanced his reputation. 'Twas of no use. He was flattened out by a gorilla, scampered over by baboons, wriggled across by snakes and other kinds of ground-hugging vermin, hopped over by toads, and *noticed* by buzzards. At last came along an enormous, slow-moving "Illinois turtle;" and that also went over him, and, unconsciously to itself—for it was an amiable creature—hurt Wendell badly in a tender spot. Wendell lay flat on his back, with his tongue pulled out upon his chin by the weight of an unusually heavy cuss which he had been unable to discharge. The claws of the turtle caught in this obstruction, split it, and from *that day* to *this* Wendell has been unable to give the full impression of his talent.

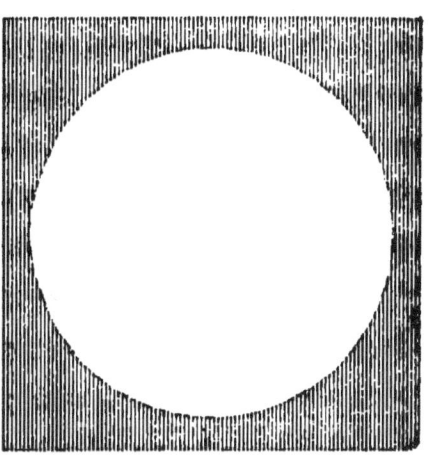

IMAGINARY PICTURE.

The Illinois turtle depriving Wendell Feelups of the power to "cuss."

The "Little Fishes" moved but a short distance in the general current, but, under the lead of a big fish, soon eddied off to one side, circled backward and around their pursuers, and finally arrived at the deserted Ark, when they all dived into the water and hid under its huge hulk, near the rudder.

Valhanghim, Admiral Sammies, and Jeff Devis had unhappy falls, tripped by the trails of the Misses Noah. The unfortunate Val was dragged some distance by Miss Hephzibah, who took after her mother—a lass of vast size and power of body.

In his unhappy flight, he attracted the attention of a Durham bull, young, wild, and full of fight, who, with its sharp horns, tore his garments most woefully.

Charles Dickens attempted to cover him with his screen, lest he should "catch cold." In this he was assisted by one Nicholas Nickleby (who had been supercargo for Captain Cook in his voyage around the world), and Captain Cuttle (who stuck his hook through the American Eagle, and gave the thing a twitch), while Bunsby delivered—hastily delivered, running—"an opinion that was an opinion;" all in vain.

It came near finishing Charles' readings, for the bull turned upon him, and he only escaped by a stratagem of one Nicholas Nickleby (who had been supercargo for Captain Cook in his voyage around the world), assisted by Captain Cuttle, and backed by an opinion from Bunsby "that was an opinion," and so remains "an opinion that was an opinion" to this present day, whatever any body else may say to the contrary, notwithstanding, *anyhow!*

Finally the trail was rent, and Val freed, only to be overtaken by the anaconda, when a tragedy ensued. Val lay panting, helpless, his clothes in shreds, "with his hands in his mouth, and his mouth in the dust," when he was leisurely slobbered over by the monster, and then swallowed.

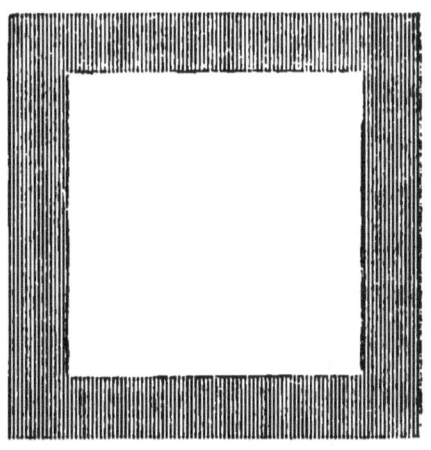

IMAGINARY PICTURE.

Val hanging being swallowed by the anaconda. Body from waist down only is seen.

But he proved too hard a morsel for the anaconda to digest. Val lived—the reptile died! What a triumph for Val!

Some hours thereafter he recovered, and was enabled to escape. This was through an heirloom left him by his grandfather, of blessed revolutionary memory—an old Barlow knife—which, fastened by an eel-string around his neck, he always carried over his heart. With this he cut a hole between the ribs of the carrion, through which he crawled, and emerged into sunlight and the waiting, anxious arms of the Democracy.

IMAGINARY PICTURE.

Presentation of the new clothes to Valhanghim by the Unterrified and Screeching, on which occasion he makes a melting speech.

The Unterrified and Screeching furnished him with an entire new suit of clothes, by dime subscriptions; hence the expresssion, *Val-hand-him-a-dime!* Understand us, they were not all dime contributions; by no means. As small sums as five cents were given, and some little folks were persuaded, in the enthusiasm of the moment, to throw in their candy pennies, but they repented, with tears in their eyes, the next time they saw a peanut stand.

IMAGINARY PICTURE.

Last appearance of Carl Rosa and Madame Parepa, and retirement from these scenes.

The presentation ceremony took place in Pike's New Opera-house. The event was celebrated by the firing of cannon, the ringing of bells, and a speech from Val, recounting his services in their behalf—his labors, persecutions, trial, expulsion as an outlaw from his native land, his return, and enthusiastic triumph over his enemies; his troubles with

Miss Hephzibah Noah, his engorgement by the anaconda, and final miraculous escape—through the means of the little heirloom left him by his grandfather, of blessed revolutionary memory—from the digestive apparatus of the monster. So touching was his narrative, that his followers wept.

And Carl Rosa played upon the violin, while Madame Parepa sang:

> "He put in his thumb,
>   And pulled out a plum,
>   And cried—
>   WHAT A GREAT BOY AM I!"

"Encore!" "Encore!" shouted the crowd, and stamped their feet, and clapped their hands, and tossed up their hats.

And Carl Rosa played upon the violin, while Madame Parepa sang:

> "I wish I was a geese,
>   All forlorn! all forlorn!
> 'Cause they 'cumulates much grease,
>   Over there! over there!
> And lives and dies in PEACE,
>   Eating corn! eating corn!"

"Encore!" again shouted the multitude; upon which Carl thrust his left hand behind him, into the right pocket of his coat, with the palm outward, and, nervously shaking the flap up and down, bowed modestly to the people; while Madame, prettily kicking the trail of her dress out of an entanglement, gave one of her graceful courtesies and winning smiles.

Then the little, delicate, flaxen-haired young Carl led away the innocent-looking, amiable, gentle-eyed, but ponderous Madame, so that neither the sweet strains of his violin, nor the delicious, bird-like voice of the beautiful lady could be heard any more.

The whole house was now "in a buzz." In all parts individuals of Milesian origin, in trembling, anxious tones, and with tearful eyes, put the query: "Would ye have yer *sister* to marry a *naygur?*" And at this the party addressed invariably raised his fist, and then brought it down with tremendous emphasis, as he replied, in a voice of solemn indignation: "*No, by thunder!*"

CHAPTER L.

Andy departs for Tennessee, escorted by the corps of " Odd Friends;" guided by a mysterious apparition in the sky, they leave, amid the tears and groans of the multitude, singing a dirge, and go marching on, marching on! the author awakes from his dream.

ANOTHER day is upon us.
Time, with his mystic wand, has brought us to the Ides of March, 1869.
We are in front of the White House.
The city is clad in mourning; the bells are tolling; minute-guns firing; flags are draped.
A dense multitude, males and females, occupy every spot.
They are attired in sable habiliments; their countenances sad, woe-stricken.
The corps of Odd Friends stand in line, under their venerable commander, Jeems Bukanning, of Old Rye Land.

They wear black scarfs; their grindstone is also draped.
Jeems has on a new pair of goggles; the glasses black; they are fastened behind by the old chain and padlock.
THE DRUM TAPS!
Two members of his corps, Shade of Jo Smith and Peregrine Pickle, step out of the ranks.
They march—march into the White House.
All await in silence.
Not a word is spoken.
Not a soul stirs.
Not a cough even is heard.
They reappear; Andy between them, in a chair formed by their hands and arms.
His arms clasp their necks.
THE DRUM TAPS!
With measured tread, they march to the grindstone.
They set him a-straddle.
A deathly pallor overspreads his countenance.
He is about to faint.
THE DRUM TAPS!
A Bladdernier steps out of the ranks.

He marches up; gives the military salute; passes up his bladder.

It is *water!* Andy turns his head in disgust.

The Bladdernier gives the parting salute; revolves on his heel; solemnly marches back to the ranks.

THE DRUM TAPS!

A colored personage, Joice Heth, steps three paces to the front.

THE DRUM TAPS!

She marches up; gives the salute; passes up a demijohn.

Andy removes the cork—*smells!*

The odor is satisfactory.

He turns up the vessel.

Every eye rests upon him, to see "how he did it."

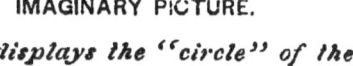
IMAGINARY PICTURE.
Andy displays the "circle" of the demijohn.

Every eye observes that the bottom of that demijohn is *a circle.*

He heeds it not.

He is done with circles.
The hole of gurgling alone attracts him.
He drinks long and strong.
The power of SUCTION survives the "wreck of matter and the crash of worlds!"
Suddenly appears in the west a small, ink-hued cloud.
It moves on like a whirlwind, enlarges as it comes, until it fills the western heavens, when it rests in silence almost overhead.
It is black and ominous; its edge of a dazzling white.
The multitude are appalled.
A terrific peal of thunder and a blinding flash of lightning momentarily stun them.
They again look.
Lo! the cloud has vanished.
In its place, miles high in air, is an immense figure, full a mile in length.
He has a weird, unearthly expression; looks like an immortal; countenance is sad, woe-begone, hard as iron.
His attire, in all but color, is like that of the Continentals of the American Revolution.

ODDS AND ENDS. 193

The coat shad-bellied and black, with white facings and trimmings; its skirt swallow-tailed, spreading apart, and very long.

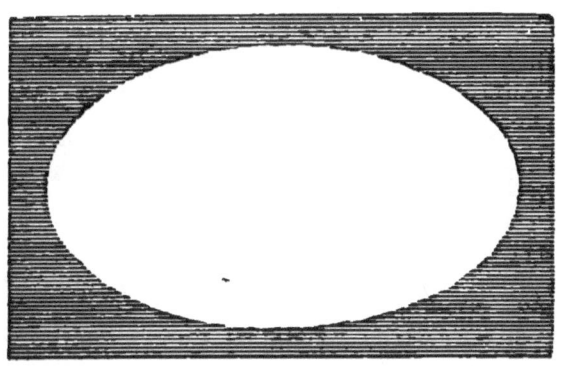

IMAGINARY PICTURE.

The awful apparition in the sky, as it stands immovable, with folded arms, and gazes down upon the terror-stricken, trembling multitude gathered in front of the White House.

The breeches are white; and he has on cavalry boots, with spurs of perhaps a quarter of a mile in length.

The cap is that of a grenadier; tall, conical, black, with white trimmings, and surmounted by a white plume, tipped with black, bobbing behind.

His hair is immense, black, and extending to the waist: perhaps in those regions of upper air there are no barber-shops.

13

This terrific presence looks down upon the crowd from eyes that sparkle like diamonds.
The pupils are a dazzling white, with a black rim.
In his hand is a wand; at the end a white streamer, bordered with black.
Across it is the single word, in black, CON-STITUTION.
This word is partly concealed by a black device—*Head of Death* and *Cross-bones!*
Every eye fastens upon this awful apparition.
For a few moments it stands immovable, with folded arms, and gazes down upon them.
Cold chills run through every soul of the vast multitude.
Their teeth all chatter.
The silence is profound, broken only by the striking together of thousands of sets of teeth.
Many faint and are borne away in the arms of friends.
Finally the apparition moves; slowly he raises the wand, points it down toward the company of Odd Friends, and describes in the air a single circle.

Then several successive jets of electricity spirts from his mouth, accompanied by a crackling noise, like sparks from an immense electrical machine.

Next the apparition revolves on his heels and points to the south-west, down toward Tennessee.

He begins to march in that direction.

He has the same singular mode of marching as Jeems; struts so much as to form a well-defined backward curve.

Each knee is, in turn, raised to the level of the thigh, and each foot alternately brought down regularly, with strong, muscular jerks.

This jerking motion is communicated to the long plume and spreading coat-tail.

The hair streams out behind.

Jeems obeys the order from his superior.

He forms his corps.

They start off, dragging Andy, a-straddle the grindstone.

His face is to the rear, the image of despair.

Jeems and his Bladderniers keep exact time to their leader up aloft.

The jerks in the sky above are simultaneous with the jerks on the earth beneath.

IMAGINARY PICTURE.

Andy, escorted by the company of Odd Friends, and a-straddle of their grindstone, leaves the White House for Tennessee. Guided by a mysterious apparition in the sky, they leave amid the tears and groans of the multitude, and singing the "Dirge of Andy." Thus they pass, in a straight line, over fields, across rivers, through forests, down valleys, over mountains, and go marching on! marching on! marching on!

As they move off, they all sing in low, wailing tones:

ODDS AND ENDS.

THE DIRGE OF ANDY.

We are marching on
  With groans and sighs;
We carry Andy,
  With tears in our eyes,
Down to Tennessee.
  O! carry Andy
Way down to Tennessee!
    O dear! O dear!
    O dear! O dear!
      O! O! O!

The circle's done,
  The Constitution dies!
It's a bee-line,
  With tears in our eyes;
Down to Tennessee!
  O! a straight bee-line,
Way down to Tennessee!
    O dear! O dear!
    O dear! O dear!
      O! O! O!

The multitude break forth in lamentations.

The men bury their faces in their hats, the females in their handkerchiefs.

Every handkerchief in that vast assemblage is "*a white handkerchief with a chain border, embroidered in scarlet silk, and the center a crescent moon, embroidered in green silk.*"

As the procession passes off, Andy again exhibits the circle of the demijohn.

He drinks long and strong.

THE POWER OF SUCTION SURVIVES "THE WRECK OF MATTER AND THE CRASH OF WORLDS!"

In a straight line the procession follows the mysterious figure on high.

Nothing obstructs its onward progress.

Over fields, across rivers, through forests, down valleys, and over mountains, it *marches on! marches on! marches on!*

To the sight of the multitude it is soon lost in the undulations of a broken country.

Not so the figure in the heavens.

It occasionally pauses, revolves slowly around on its heel, describes with its wand a single circle in the air, jets of electricity spirt from its mouth, it again revolves, points down toward the south-west, and then *marches on! marches on! marches on!*

The day wanes.

The mysterious figure is many, many miles away.

At once, as if by magic, a white cloud appears just beyond him, not rounding, cumulus, with varied tints of shade, but all of one uniform hue, like a huge white sheet stretched in front.

Its upper edge is a straight, horizontal line across the heavens, above which stands out the sky, distinct and clear.

He marches into it and disappears.

A moment later, it is broken, and resolves itself into an immense mass of pearly-white, steam-like vapor, then vanishes.

Again the mysterious figure in the sky appears.

Lo! beside him stands another apparition—a jet-black horse of beautiful proportions; prancing, restless, full of life.

The two are projected in bold relief against the cold, gray sky.

He mounts.

ODDS AND ENDS.

The animal apparition flies around with him.
It seems miraculous that he can remain upon this fiery charger.
Continuous jets of electricity issue from his mouth, as though he was trying to soothe its vivacity.

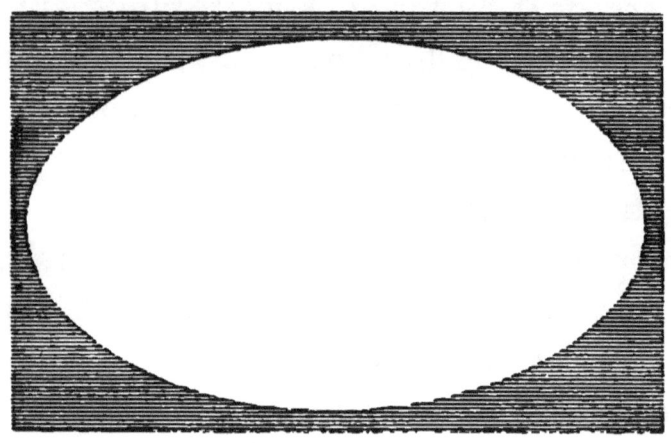

IMAGINARY PICTURE.

The mysterious apparition in the sky is joined by another apparition, that of a horse, when he goes riding on! riding on! riding on!

Finally he has him under control.
Then he puts spurs to his flank.
Holding the wand upright at arm's length in front of him, while the streamer stretches far behind, he gallops an immense circle in the air.

It can not be less than sixty miles.
A few moments suffice for its completion.
Then he heads toward the south-west, and goes slowly *riding on! riding on! riding on!*
The day closes.
Night is present.
The sky in the south-west assumes a lurid, unearthly glare.
Against this, gradually diminishing in apparent size by distance, yet in sharp relief, is the apparition, weird-like, *riding on! riding on! riding on!*
Through the long watches of the night, the people stand gazing upon it, awe-stricken, with blanched cheeks and quivering nerves, until the Great Sun, in its majestic course, shoots forth its gladdening beams, when it begins *fading away! fading away! fading away!*
In a few moments it is an impalpable mist; its outline lost.
Then it vanishes—the precise moment none can tell—and is seen no more forever!

"Halloo! who's there?"

"It's me, Doᣳther!"

"Ho! you, Bridget? What do you want?"

"The load of coal yer Honor bo't yestherday has come, an' the mon wants ye to sign the *tayke-it!*"

My long dream was thus abruptly broken and ended by the voice and knock at my door of Bridget, our great, stalwart Queen of Frysome—tall as a grenadier, strong as a giant, faithful to us as an attached New Foundland to his master—from that woe-stricken isle of the ocean which that hard, dogmatic old curmudgeon, JOHN BULL, with his massive jaws, has clutched by the throat between him and sunset, and there mercilessly *squeezes, squeezes, squeezes,* until its LIFE-BLOOD *oozes, oozes, oozes* from every pore, runs into the Atlantic a broad, living stream, flows across its wide expanse, and washes upon our shores!

"Give us your great, shaggy PAW! hearty, honest, bluff old JOHN BULL!

"We did you wrong to call you hard names!

"You served PAT right—you did—to seize him by the throat, squeeze hard, and then to finish by turning him around and swinging in a solid kick that sent him 'scooting' clear across the Atlantic!

IMAGINARY PICTURE.

The life-blood of Ireland as it oozes, oozes, oozes from every pore, runs into the Atlantic a broad, living stream, flows across its wide expanse, and washes upon our shores!

"Pat *loves* you for it—he does! he saw how you enjoyed it, and *aches, aches* to bestow like benefits!

"*Imitation*, John, is the greatest flattery!

"John, you are Pat's ideal of the right thing!

"Pat 'goes in' for the 'Dimmycratic

ODDS AND ENDS.

tayk-it,' so he can keep the ball moving—swing *his* boot-toes into SAMBO!

"Who knows but he may yet get up a high frolic in the line of a huge bonfire?—burn an ORPHAN ASYLUM of 'little ebonies!'

IMAGINARY PICTURE.

Orphan asylum in flames. *"Fun to see the 'little ebonies' scamper out, and hear 'em scream!—hear 'em scream!"*

"John, when this *does* take place, we must all be present, unite in the sport, tap the whisky-barrel, bring out the big fiddle, join all hands in a great ring, and have a jolly dance around the flames! Won't it be fun

ODDS AND ENDS. 205

to see the little ebonies scamper out, and hear 'em *scream!*—hear 'em *scream!*"

We all, if we do n't find any body to kick, can to "snub," especially if we are a little ways up, and have our fill of the comforts and pleasures. To snub enhances one's self-complacency, adds to our respectability, is among the utilities! Plenty of folks are all around us who, having a hard time here, it should be our aim to make more miserable, by giving the "cold shoulder;" we must *snub 'em!— snub 'em!*

The Great Husbandman scatters his freshly-created souls broadcast, irrespective of the bodies into which they may drop and germinate, so that in the humblest conditions are often exquisitely delicate spirits, who pant to extricate themselves from the mire and brambles by which their footsteps are impeded and their pathway hedged; to wander in the groves, beside the brooks; to hear the voices of the winds, and the murmuring of the waters over the pebbles. Young man and young woman, such are about you every-where. As it is your duty, *snub 'em! snub 'em!*

* * * * * * * *

We had an awful dream!

If you want a similar experience, partake late at night of a hearty supper of coppery oysters, and, perhaps, you too may swallow some copperheads!

Even then you can't have as horrid a dream as we had. Copperheads are not so venomous as they were, and are growing less and less venomous every day!

May the time soon arrive when the venom will be all out of them, and they changed into the kind called by little children "good snakes!"

For the present they should be "poked up" with sticks. We have high authority for this—"THE SEED OF WOMAN SHALL BRUISE THE SERPENT'S HEAD."

CHAPTER M.

In which burlesque and satire are dropped, and the reader led to pause and reflect: "What are we?" "Where do we stand?" "Whither are we tending?"

BURLESQUE and satire embrace within their legitimate field the follies, vices, and idiosyncracies of public men, communities, and policies. Error, when impregnable to reason, is often vanquished by a laugh.

We have given some range to our imagination in the presentation of the grotesque, absurd, and impossible in connection with the actualities of our time.

Some intellects are so literal that such associations are repulsive, while others relish them with a zest akin to that which childhood derives from tales of genii and fairies. If, however, the most matter-of-fact minds should be deprived of all the creations of fancy, a deep vacuum would be made in their delights.

Personally we have enjoyed originating this book. It was in us, and made such strong implorations to depart, that we finally said, "Go, and peace be with you!" But we had no thought that the little fellow would grow so much in the few weeks we knew him, and in which we prepared him for his trip.

The idea of going on a journey and seeing the world has so exhilarated him, that he has attained an unexpected expansion. He has come up at once from short frocks and slippers into a roundabout and pantaloons, with high-heeled boots, adorned by illuminated tops.

We now propose to devote a few terminating pages to a higher range of expression. It violates the canons of literature to go from the humorous to the serious, although in the stream of our lives they meet continually, and form opposing contrasts. Our excuse is, that the habit of our mind leads us to discard precedents.

> "The bride shall have the stock,
> The groom the wall;
> All old customs will I turn and change,
> And call it reformation,"

are lines which, without exactly fitting our niche, express a thought that in some degree touches a point or so in it.

In the terrible state of morals now existing in our country—the natural result of a long war and the sudden inflation of our currency—it becomes us all to pause, elevate our thoughts from the absorbing details of daily life, and take a broad view of our situation; to solemnly inquire:

"What are we?"
"Where do we stand?"
"Whither are we tending?"

It is to assist some minds in doing this, that otherwise would not be reached, that we place here ideas that were in us demanding utterance:

Another day, with its cares and duties, is ushered upon our land.
THIS DAY!
Mean spirits fawn in the light of power!
Harsh natures crush the weak!
Scandal spirts out bitterness!
Jealousy burns in vile bosoms!

Pride struts on the gains of oppression!
Cant and Hypocrisy steal the garb of Religion!
Merchants adulterate their goods, or temporarily lower their prices to crush their weaker brothers!
Avarice drives hard bargains with ignorance, and then boasts of its regard for the sacredness of contracts!
Pettifoggers stir up contention!
Quacks found palaces on human woes!
Monopolies bribe legislatures and municipalities!
Railroad officers cheat stockholders!
Vanity beggars families!
Demagogues lure the simple ones!
Modest merit quails in the presence of brazen pretense!
Fiends, with soft tongues and wily manners, plot the ruin of trusting innocence!
And HELL CHUCKLES!
Oh! it is a horrible world!

THIS DAY!
Joy kindles loving hearts!
Mothers rejoice over their first-born!

Sons and daughters, dutiful, gladden paternal hearths!
Noble souls loathe ignoble deeds!
Charity extends her helping hand to the suffering!
Kind words are dispensed, and prove a balm to anguished spirits!
The pure in heart hunger and thirst after perfection!
And HEAVEN SMILES!
Oh! it is a beautiful world!

THIS NIGHT!

In a remote, desolate, uninhabited, wilderness country, on the topmost point of a lofty mountain, stands a MAN—*alone!* Miles below him is the whole earth; that summit the only one above the general level.

He looks down upon the world, enshrouded in gloom. It appears like an immense basin; its rim the horizon line, which, in its complete circumference, stands, rising up to his view, hard, sharply-defined against the midnight sky.

The vast dome of heaven, from the rarity

of the air, is black as ink; and upon this background the stars project with a clearness and brilliancy no words can express.

IMAGINARY PICTURE.

An unknown man on the summit of a lofty mountain, in a distant, wilderness country. Time, night. Light from myriads of far away, unknown worlds pierce his very soul, and he feels the awful presence of the INFINITE!

As he stands there alone, gazing, his cheeks blanch with awe. Light from myriads of far away, unknown worlds pierce his very soul, and he feels the awful presence of the INFINITE!

And what is MAN? An atom, ignorant even of himself! The greatest only large enough to fill a single grave! His life is brief—brief, like the transient shadow formed by the wheat, as it is undulated in the gentle wind of summer!

Man puts his hand upon his heart:
"Is he there?"
"No!"
He puts his hand upon his forehead:
"Is he there?"
"No!"
He looks in a mirror:
"And what does he see?"

Only his body, the casement of his soul. But the human soul, the entity—the *man himself*—no mortal ever saw! It is only by manifestations from this body of ours that we know there is such an existence as a human soul, that there is such an existence as a man.

If the souls of men walked the earth as do their bodies, how quickly would our estimate of individuals change! Many a man who now occupies and has risen to a place of power, through the exercise of abhorrent qualities, would stand out in loathsome deformity; so repulsive, disgusting, that we should turn from him with a shudder! Many a one in the lowly ranks of life would be to us an object of beauty, of tender, loving interest.

Life consists only of sensations. To its happiness three things are necessary:

1. A good body—that is, health.
2. Employment for the intellect.
3. Employment for the heart.

The last is the first. Without heart-joys, life is valueless. These come only through an eye open loving to the works of God in Nature; an eye open loving to the works of God in Man. This says to the humblest:

"*Thou art my* BROTHER *and my* SISTER! Here's my hand, and we'll help you along in this little, short journey we are taking together, this strange medley of joy, and woe, and mystery—LIFE!"

And when man does this, there comes to him a sweet peace, a joy that fills his soul, and makes his cup of existence a delicious beverage ever present to his lips, for he is in *harmony* with God!

OUR NATION IS NOW SUFFERING FOR HER CRIMES! The wounds from the recently plucked barb are still rankling in her heart! In the decrees of the Eternal there is no escape from the violation of law. Sooner or later, Justice lets down from the skies her great, pearly-white balances, tries iniquity, and, according to its weight, pronounces sentence!

Four millions of our people—a long-suffering, humble people, whose very weakness should have won our sympathies—have been crushed by organized human law. It has been forbidden to allow the development of the only quality that separates man from the brute—*intellect*. This is the awful nameless CRIME AGAINST THE HUMAN SOUL!

In part we have expiated this by the death of half a million of young men, the very flower of our land—enough to fill a triple line of coffins from the capitol of our nation to Richmond, the capitol of the would-be assassins of Liberty.

To rob the nation of the means to complete the expiation of her crimes, by doing justice in the future to those whom she has wronged, the means which have been paid for in BLOOD, is now the attempt of a powerful organization, which stretches over the wide expanse of our vast country.

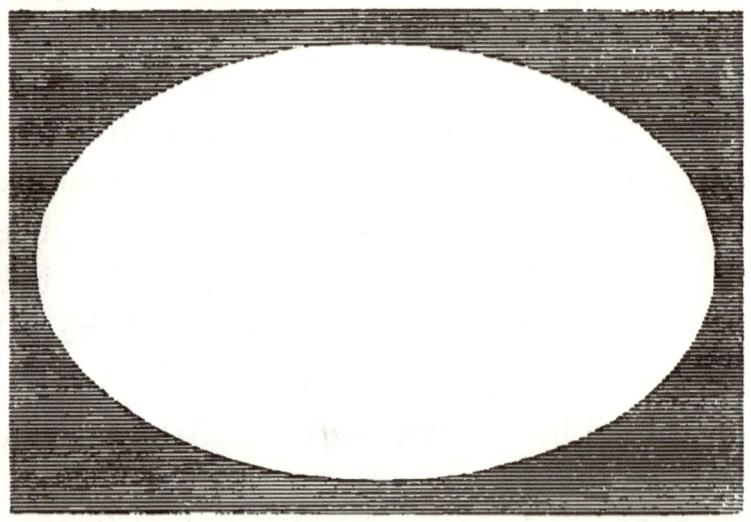

IMAGINARY PICTURE.

The triple line of coffins of the nation's slain extending from Washington to Richmond.

If the spirits of our slain could arise from their graves, with their bodies gashed and gory, would they not point to their wounds and thus implore us?

"FIGHT THE WRONG! FIGHT THE WRONG! If not for your own sakes, for you will soon pass away, yet for the sake of the humble, ignorant, and wonderfully patient people whom you have injured; for the sake of the great future; for the sake of the little ones whose lithe figures and sweet, trusting faces are upturned to you and meet you everywhere—in the streets, at public gatherings, and around your own hearthstones!"

* * * * * * * *

We present an even number of—
Odd Figures: 3, 5, 7, 9.
A Man.
A Glove.
A Woman.
A Slipper.
A Leaf.
A Stone.

Each of the above is a subject for a book, for endless volumes: for every idea is connected with every other idea; every truth with every other truth; and all ideas and all truths keep evil company, travel with numerous errors and falsehoods. We do not enlarge upon these, but simply leave the reader to think a discourse from either at option.

But Remember!

After this little book is read and forgotten, and its uses forgotten—for nothing, not even folly, is in vain;

After we discover that we are but weaklings, the clearest-eyed only able to dimly discern the outer edges of knowledge;

After we perceive that from chaos comes order; from incongruity, congruity; from barbarism, civilization; from ignorance, wisdom; from learning, humility; that in the eternal progress we shall approach nearer and nearer all truth, but never fully reach it;

After we learn there are no great things and no small things; that the vast is but an aggregation of the minute; that the minute itself surpasses comprehension; that to be

"Pleased with a rattle, tickled with a straw,"

is alike the pursuit and the enjoyment of the child and the man, the rattle and the straw only varying with each, and each and all are but children together—simple, prejudiced, and ignorant;

After we see that to live life wisely is to develop this soul of ours here in harmony with Eternal Law; to gather from the present, our only possession, its fruition; to exult that we are born into an existence where wonders never cease; where there is ever beauty to elevate; wherever, by kind acts and tender words, our souls can be expanded; while over all, protecting all, is the GREAT MYSTERY and the GREAT LOVE;

After a million of years have come and gone—

REMEMBER!

The sun *may* somewhere continue to rise!

New souls to be created, and experience scenes with us now passing!

Voices of children to be heard!

Youths and maidens to dream the sweet dream their parents once dreamed!

Families to nestle under protecting roofs!

Old age to sit serene in the mellow twilight!

The funeral bell to awe, as its single note

strikes in the tower, and then fainting, dies trembling away!

Music to thrill with a foretaste of the bliss that awaits on immortality!

Mortal agony to be sustained through the hope of immortal joy!

Hearts to expand through sacrifice!

Grief to soften and purify!

Snow, in delicate, undulating lines, to envelop landscapes with purity!

Laughter to relieve from care!

Light to gladden and illuminate the Universe!

Flowers to delight by perfumes, tints, and forms!

Dew-drops to glisten!

Mountains to pierce the sky!

Leaves to dance in gentle zephyrs!

Earth, air, and sea to pour forth unceasing melody!

Deserts to lay in solitude!

Shadows to flit over fields and mountain sides!

Oceans to roll in grandeur!

Clouds to float softly in summer skies!

Night made sublime by light from unknown, far-away worlds!

Forests to cover vast tracts unknown to man!

Wavelets to break upon curving sands!

Brooks to leap and laugh!

The rainbow to span the heavens in an arch of glory!

Thunder to crash and echo!

Grain to bend in the breeze, and grow golden for the harvest!

Fruits to ripen and become luscious!

Pines to moan in weird-like, Æolian strains!

Bees to hum among clover blossoms!

Lambs to skip in green pastures!

Kittens to play around firesides!

Cows to graze down in the meadows, and recline by the margin of cool waters!

The crimson-speckled trout to lie secreted in their clear, deep, liquid haunts!

The soft clouds of night to play hide-and-seek with the moon!

Mossy branches to bend over and lave in pure waters!

Morning and evening shadows to lay long over landscapes!

Fawns to bound through forest glades!

Cool, leafy groves to invite to repose from noonday heats!

Snow-hued clouds to be banked up against the blue skies of summer!

Mist to envelop landscapes, and as the early light of morning darts forth, convert them into isles and oceans of wondrous and evanescent glory!

Thus Nature will entrance by her variety, soothe by her tranquillity, delight by her beauty, fill and inspire by her grandeur, sadden and purify by her gloom, and elevate and awe by her sublimity!

The GREAT MYSTERY *may* create all this!

Where, then, will we be?

That will not be the end. The Eternal Mind requires eternal use; and as there never was the beginning, so never can be the end.

Forever will be poured forth sweet strains; forever will be warbled delicious melodies; forever will mountain tops pierce the skies; forever will oceans roll in grandeur; forever will the thunders crash and give their awful echoes; and the stars and the angels will forever unceasingly sing the sublime music of the Universe, the GREAT MYSTERY, and the GREAT LOVE; and forever will be the morning song of creation—worlds upon worlds, worlds upon worlds, worlds without end!

Thus, the GRAND REFRAIN OF THE UNIVERSE—*Forever!*

Therefore forever will hearts bound with glorious emotion; forever will the sweet tears of sympathy and joy start, and the nerves thrill, as the successive waves of delicious sensation strike and pass over the delicate, vibrating chords of the immortal soul!

Thus, HEART JOYS—*Forever!*

What an inheritance ours, even this brief life! No wonder the soul shrinks from the dread unknown! None have returned thence! Yes! ONE has! And HE—*so sad, so tender, so compassionate*, that the hearts of the pure melt at the thought!—*so sad, so tender, so compassionate*, for the weak, the lowly, the suffering!—*so sad, so tender, so compassionate*—CHRIST THE CRUCIFIED!

THE END.

www.ingramcontent.com/pod-product-compliance
Lightning Source LLC
Chambersburg PA
CBHW021835230426
43669CB00008B/978